Innocent Targets

When Terrorism Comes to School

Michael and Chris Dorn

Innocent Targets – When Terrorism Comes to School
©2011 by Michael Dorn and Chris Dorn

Edited by Robert Fanney

Safe Havens International, Inc., an IRS approved non profit school safety center
www.safehavensinternational.org
www.schoolterrorism.com
www.weakfish.org

ISBN 10: 0-9741240-1-X
ISBN 13: 978-0-9741240-1-8
LCCN 2004097931

Book and cover design by Pamela Terry, Opus 1 Design
www.Opus1design.com

Cover photograph by Ray Nichols

Printed in Canada
Fourth Printing, Hardcover, December, 2010

Dedication

This book is dedicated to the children, teachers and parents who have been ruthlessly murdered by terrorists around the world. Our hearts also go out to the survivors they left behind.

Disclaimer

The information presented in this book is designed to provide general background for the creation of a reasonably safe school climate. Readers should be aware that school and youth service professionals should seek the advice of competent legal counsel and local public safety, risk management and emergency management personnel prior to implementation of any new programs or techniques, especially those that may have legal or safety implications. Methods of implementing procedures, programs and strategies outlined in this book are obviously beyond the control of the authors. Therefore, the authors, editor and Safe Havens International Inc. assume no liability for the application of any concepts described in this book.

ABOUT THE AUTHORS

Michael Dorn

Michael Dorn is the Executive Director of Safe Havens International Inc., a non profit school safety center. Under a unique contract for Safe Havens, he also serves as the Senior Public Safety and Emergency Management Consultant for Jane's Consultancy. Jane's selected Michael after an international search for the world's top school safety expert to represent their company's nine offices around the world. Globally recognized with over 105 years of experience, Jane's is widely regarded as the world's leading provider of defense, security and school safety information. During his twenty year campus law enforcement career, he served with the Mercer University Police Department rising from the rank of Police Officer to the rank of Lieutenant before being appointed as a school district police chief at the age of twenty seven. The school system police department he led is widely used as a model school law enforcement program by many agencies including the United States Departments of Education and Justice.

After ten years as chief of police, he was selected to serve as the School Safety Specialist for the Georgia Emergency Management Agency – Office of the Governor and in that capacity was the state's top school safety expert. After the horrendous events of September 11th, 2001, the agency was designated as part of the Georgia Office of Homeland Security. He was selected as the State Antiterrorism Planner in the spring of 2003 and then as the Lead Program Manager for the Terrorism Emergency Response and Preparedness Division a few months later. He resigned from his position with the Office of Homeland Security when he was selected by Jane's in February, 2004.

He has authored and co-authored twenty books on school safety including the 450 page *Jane's Safe School Planning Guide for All Hazards* – the most comprehensive book published to date on school safety. He pens columns for *School Planning and Management, Today's School, Campus Safety, School Transportation News* and *College Planning and Management* magazines.

More than 50,000 copies of his training videos and DVDs are in use by school, police and intelligence officials in more than 20 countries. The FBI, U.S. Secret Service, Transportation Security Administration, Federal Emergency Management Agency, Israel Police, and British intelligence and security services have utilized his videos and DVDs.

He has bachelor's and master's degrees from Mercer University, is a graduate of the prestigious eleven week FBI National Academy Program at Quantico, Virginia and was selected for a fellowship from Georgia State University to train in Israel through the Georgia International Law Enforcement Exchange Program (GILEE). During his fourteen day stay in Israel, He received advanced antiterrorism and counterterrorism training and briefings from the Israel Police, Israel Defense Forces and the Mossad. He has also received advanced antiterrorism training from the FBI, Bureau of Alcohol, Tobacco and Firearms, Georgia Public Safety Training Center and the Georgia Police Academy.

Chris Dorn

Michael Dorn's son Chris is a student at Georgia Tech. He has co-authored two short books on school safety and has astounded audiences at professional conferences in more than 20 states with his concealed weapons demonstrations, keynote presentations and breakout sessions. While only twenty one years old, he has already presented at such unique places as Opryland, Disney World, Montana State University, the Kansas Highway Patrol Academy, and the Oklahoma Governor's Mansion. Chris has trained police officers, police chiefs, school superintendents, teachers, bus drivers, and other school employees at state, national and international conferences around the nation. While still in high school he was asked to provide his weapons concealment demonstration for a group of high ranking police officials from Israel through the GILEE program. Chris has appeared in two of the above mentioned training videos and has another training video and his first self published book, both on drug identification in schools, that are scheduled for completion in spring, 2005. Chris is very well known in the school safety community with his demonstrations having been featured on *Larry King Live*, *The Sally Jesse Raphael Show*, *Good Morning America*, *ABC World News Tonight With Peter Jennings* and in the United Artists movie *Bowling For Columbine* (in a video clip used without his permission). Chris also serves as a member of the Jane's Consultancy team.

And the editor
Robert Marston Fanney

Robert is currently the Editor and Chief of *Chemistry Business Magazine* with a circulation in excess of 10,000. He is also a former

Content Developer, Editor, and Consultant for *Jane's Information Group*. Rob was the Editor and Project Manager for *Jane's Safe School Planning Guide for All Hazards*, *Jane's School Safety Handbook*, *Jane's Teacher's Safety Handbook*, *Jane's Chem-bio Handbook*, *Jane's Chem-bio Handbook International*, *Jane's Chem-bio Web*, *Jane's CopCase* and *Jane's World Insurgency and Terrorism*. At Jane's Rob also served as Coordinating Editor for all public safety and emerging threats products including the *Chem-bio Defense Guidebook* and *Counterterrorism*. During the anthrax letter mailings in 2002, Rob briefed the U.S. Postal Service on mail handling procedures to mitigate the risk posed by Chem-bio materials during that critical time and has since worked with such world-renowned experts as Ken Alibek, Rohan Gunaratna, Marleen Wong, Gregory Thomas and Michael Dorn. Rob has also spoken at the Community Policing Through Environmental Design Conference in Calgary Canada. In addition to his extensive editorial and analysis experience, Rob has written over sixty magazine articles, has authored a critical white paper on industry security, drafted a six hundred page predictive technology analysis for the *Alvin Toffler Association*, and was co-author of the ground-breaking *Jane's Citizen's Safety Guide*. He is a former Intelligence Analyst, National Guardsman as well as Police Officer for Naval Security Force (NSF). Rob is currently launching a publishing company while working on his first major novel which is due out in 2005.

Other books authored or co-authored by Michael and Chris Dorn:

High as a Kite, Grownups Guide to Drugs and Drug Paraphernalia (working title) by Chris Dorn, due for publication in 2005, Safe Havens International Inc.
www.thedrugbook.com

Let None Learn In Fear, due for publication in 2005, Safe Havens International Inc.
www.weakfish.org

Jane's Safe Schools Planning Guide for All Hazards
Jane's Teacher Safety Guide
Jane's School Safety Handbook: 2nd Ed.
www.janes.com or 1-800-824-0768

School/Law Enforcement Partnerships: A Guide to Police Work in Schools, Ram Publishing.
www.weakfish.org

Policing and Crime Prevention, Edited by Deborah Mitchell Robinson, Prentice Hall.
www.prenhall.com/policestore

School Safety Essentials series of short books, LRP Publishing.
1-800-341-7874, ext. 275.

> Developing Emergency Operations Plans
> Creating Safe Learning Environments
> Writing Successful Grant Proposals
> Creating Secure School Safety Zones
> Forming School-to-Student Partnerships
> Reuniting Students and Parents When a Crisis Hits
> Handling Bomb Threats
> Developing School Safety Plans
> Conducting Tactical Site Surveys
> Performing Daily Safety Sweeps
> Developing School Crisis Teams
> Reducing Weapons in Your School

Warriors: On Living with Courage, Discipline, and Honor, edited by Loren W. Christensen, Paladin Press, 1-303-443-7250.

"He who protects everything, protects nothing."

—Sun Tzu
The Art of War

ACKNOWLEDGEMENTS

We would like to express our gratitude to the people who have made this book possible and who have provided us with support and motivation over time. First, we would like to express our deepest thanks to the experts quoted in the text who were so generous with their time. Being top experts, these individuals are all extremely busy spending a considerable amount of time traveling the globe to share their extensive knowledge. Their kindness in taking time from their hectic schedules shall not be forgotten.

We likewise appreciate the many dedicated staff members at Jane's who have been so incredibly supportive of schools in the development of their school safety publications and in the delivery of high quality consulting services to schools and communities through Jane's Consultancy. While space does not permit us to thank the numerous Jane's employees who have helped us, we would like to particularly mention three people who have spearheaded the company's efforts to make schools safer: in the Virginia office, Jim Tinsley, Consultancy Manager and Scott Hayes, The Director of Public Safety have become close friends as well as respected colleagues. Jo Moon, the Chief Sales and Marketing Officer working out of the corporate headquarters in England, has also been instrumental in building a consultancy focused on helping schools and communities learn to internalize expertise so they can steadily improve safety without perpetual reliance on private consultants. The Jane's approach to school safety consulting is in stark contrast to many firms who try to create a situation of long term reliance with school systems that can rarely afford to fiscally support this approach.

We would also like to express our support for the many local, state and federal government officials who have worked steadfastly to make our schools safer and more prepared for all hazards, including terrorism. Of particular note, Bill Modzeleski, the Associate Deputy Under-Secretary for the Office of Safe and Drug-Free Schools in the United States Department of Education, has earned our respect as a staunch and tireless advocate for the children.

Chris would like to thank those who helped him learn how to research and write, especially Mr. Stanford Brown, his high school history teacher. Without the dedication and guidance of teachers like Mr. Brown and others in Central High School's International Baccalaureate Program, Chris would not be where he is today. He would also like to thank his parents for guiding him and allowing him to make mistakes and learn in his own way.

TABLE OF CONTENTS

Lt. Col. Dave Grossman is a former West Point psychology professor, Professor of Military Science, and an Army Ranger who is the author of *On Combat* (which was nominated for a Pulitzer Prize), *On Killing* (with Loren Christensen), and *Stop Teaching Our Kids to Kill* (with Gloria DeGaetano). Col. Grossman's work has been translated into many languages, and his books are required or recommended reading in colleges, military academies, and police academies around the world, to include the U.S. Marine Corps Commandant's reading list and the FBI Academy reading list. His research was cited by the President of the United States in a national address after the Littleton, Colorado school shootings, and he has testified before the U.S. Senate, the U.S. Congress, and numerous state legislatures. He has served as an expert witness and consultant in state and Federal courts, to include UNITED STATES vs. TIMOTHY MCVEIGH. He helped train mental health professionals after the Jonesboro school shootings, and he was also involved in counseling or court cases in the aftermath of the Paducah, Springfield, and Littleton school shootings. He has been called upon to write the entry on "Aggression and Violence" in the *Oxford Companion to American Military History*, three entries in the *Academic Press Encyclopedia of Violence, Peace and Conflict* and has presented papers before the national conventions of the American Medical Association, the American Psychiatric Association, the American Psychological Association, and the American Academy of Pediatrics. Today he is the director of the Killology Research Group (www.killology.com), and in the wake of the 9/11 terrorist attacks he has been on the road almost 300 days a year, training elite military and law enforcement organizations worldwide about the reality of combat, and he has written extensively on the terrorist threat with articles published in the *Harvard Journal of Law and Public Policy* and many leading law enforcement journals.

FOREWORD

The possibility of a mass murder of school children by terrorists is very real. It has happened in many nations already, and terrorists have been able to see the impact school violence has already had in America. The worst terrorist act in modern Russian history was the Beslan school massacre. One of the most tragic and devastating terrorist acts in Israel was the Ma'alot school massacre. Turkey had over 300 schools destroyed in their battle against terrorists. These are just some of the tragic and horrific terrorist attacks upon schools that have occurred around the globe, and all of these attacks are outlined in detail in this book.

But, the sky is not falling. Terrorist attacks on schools are relatively rare, and this is only one of many things that terrorists could do to us. If we overreact, if we change our way of life because of the threat of school massacres, then we give way to fear and the terrorists get the victory they desire without having to fire a shot.

So, how do you strike a balance between preparing for an unthinkable horror without giving way to unreasoned fear?

That is exactly what Michael and Chris Dorn have done in this book.

First, you need to understand that the credentials of the authors, and the experts they have called upon to assist in this book are of the very highest possible caliber.

I have been a co-trainer with Michael Dorn and his son on several occasions. I often speak to audiences about Michael Dorn's work in my presentations, and I always refer to him as "our nation's leading expert on school safety." Michael Dorn has solid experience as a leader, a consultant, an author, and an expert in both a government school safety center and a government antiterrorism program. In addition, Michael Dorn has extensive experience as a law enforcement officer and a law enforcement leader. To add to his own direct, personal expertise, he has called upon the world's leading experts to assist in writing this book. I am honored that Michael invited me to make a small contribution to this important work.

Second, you need to know that this is not an alarmist book. This book joins the ranks of Gavin de Becker's classics, *The Gift of Fear*, *Protecting the Gift*, and *Fear Less* in presenting a valuable, balanced assessment of a frightening subject without fear-mongering.

It is vital that we respond to this potential threat in a measured, realistic, balanced fashion. Too much fear or any fear-mongering will play into the hands of those who want to do us harm. If we are not careful, those who wish to destroy our way of life could do so without having to make an actual terrorist attack. Providing a balanced, reasoned, informed, "all hazards" approach is one of the great contributions of this book.

Thus, while keeping the matter in proper perspective, we need to understand how destructive a school massacre in the U.S. could be. A successful school massacre by terrorists here in the U.S. could force us to be like Israel, diverting vast resources to protecting our kids. How could we not? It is our moral responsibility to keep those kids safe.

Consider the way we approach fire safety in schools. The probability of a student being killed or seriously injured by violence is significantly greater than the probability of being killed or seriously injured by fire. No child has been killed by school fire in North America in over a quarter of a century. Compare this to the fact that, in any given year in our schools, dozens of students and employees are killed by acts of violence. These are usually random acts of violence, or shootings by students as opposed to acts of terrorism, but the defense against terrorist attacks in our schools, as outlined in this book, is largely the same as the defense against conventional school shootings.

Thus, our children are dozens of times more likely to be killed by violence than fire, and thousands of times more likely to be seriously injured by violence as compared to fire. And yet, in any school you can look around and see fire sprinklers, smoke alarms, fire exits, and fire extinguishers. If we can spend all that money and time preparing for fire (and we should, since every life is precious), shouldn't we spend time and money preparing for the thing that is far more likely to kill or injure a child?

The most negligent, unprofessional, obscene words anyone can ever say are, "It will never happen here." Imagine the firefighter saying, "There will never be a fire in this building, and we don't need those fire extinguishers."

When someone says, "Do you really think there will be a terrorist act or a school shooting here?" I just point to the fire exit and say, "Do you really think there will be a fire here? Statistically speaking, it is very unlikely that there would ever be a fire here. But we would be morally, criminally negligent if we did not prepare for the possibility. And the same is far, far more true of school violence."

In an article published in the Harvard Journal of Law and Public Policy, my co-author and I stated that if a series of active shooter terrorist attacks happen in the U.S. as they have in Israel, then we will arm our selves and get on with life just like Israel. But, you can't arm the kids! Even Israel can't arm their children, and if a major terrorist attack on a school (or worse, several schools at once) is successful, the terrorists can impact every family and every school in America, disrupting our economy and way of life unlike any other attack has ever done. It is our job to prevent that and to protect our kids, and this book is a key tool to make that possible.

It was about a month after the 9-11 terrorist attacks, and I was training a group of special operations troops who were headed off to Afghanistan. A Special Forces (Green Beret) sergeant came up to me during one of the breaks and said, "Colonel, we're going to Afghanistan, and we're gonna kick their tails. While we're over there, you tell all those folks you teach, don't let them come kill our kids."

Our servicemen are over there dying for us, every day, trying to close down the terrorist camps, to keep the terrorists on the run, to keep them on the defense, or as one marine put it, "To keep it the hell over there!" They believe in what they are doing. And they only ask one thing: "Watch my back, do your job ... don't let them come kill my kids." That is what this book is about. This book is a key tool to help keep our kids and our nation safe.

On the night of the school massacre at Westside Middle School in Jonesboro, Arkansas, I was at the school helping to train the mental health professionals who would work with the teachers and students in the coming days. As a former West Point Psychology Professor and one of the U.S. Army's experts on PTSD, I was applying the lessons of mass critical incident debriefings learned on the battlefield to my home town.

A counselor who had been working at the hospital came to the school that night, and she told us a story that brought us all to tears. Clergy and counselors were working in small groups in the hospital waiting room, comforting the groups of relatives and friends of more than a dozen shooting victims. They noticed one woman who had been sitting silently, alone, in the midst of the crowd. A counselor went up to the woman, took her hand, and said, "Can I help you?"

Sitting there in absolute psychological and physiological shock she said, "I'm the mother of one of the girls who was killed today. They called me, and said my little girl is dead. I just came to find out how I can get my little girl back. How do I get her body back?"

She had no friends, no husband, no family with her as she sat in the hospital, alone and stunned by her loss. But the body had been taken to Little Rock, 100 miles away, for an autopsy and she was told that the authorities would contact her when they were finished with the body, then she could tell them what funeral home to send the body to. After being told this, in her dazed mind her very next comment was, "Funeral home? Funeral home? We can't afford a funeral. We can't even afford a funeral."

That little girl was truly all that woman had in the world. There were no friends, no family, no husband. There was just a mama, and her little girl. That morning she hugged her little girl, alive and warm and vital, the most precious thing on the face of the Earth... for the last time. And that night, all she wanted in all the world was to wrap her baby's cold body in a blanket and take her home.

Every day, millions of parents hug millions of kids, their most precious possession, the most precious thing on the face of the Earth, and they send those kids to school, trusting us to keep them alive. This is the most important thing any society can do: protect our young.

So don't just read this book, study it. Study it and apply it. Be like the firefighter: Put the risk in perspective, pray that it will never happen, know that it could happen, and work with all your heart and soul to prevent it from happening. It could be your child's life that you save.

Lt. Col. Dave Grossman, U.S. Army (Ret.)
Director, Killology Research Group
www.killology.com

INTRODUCTION

The gunman fired relentlessly into the bodies of innocent children and adults on the bus. Moments after the attack, nine children and three adults lay motionless and nineteen more were grievously wounded. The victim's suffering would only be compounded by that of their loved ones, the State of Israel, and the world community as people struggled to understand how any person, no matter how ruthless, could target helpless children in an act of terrorism.

This tragic massacre occurred on May 8, 1970. It was one of the first of what would become a long, though intermittent, series of incidents where terrorists directly targeted schools, school buses and school children with acts of violence. In addition to terrorism specifically targeting schools and children, major terrorist attacks on targets near schools have resulted in school children falling into the line of fire. Whether incidentally, or by design, in many of these brutal attacks, innocent children have been killed, seriously injured, or emotionally scarred.

Teachers who have dedicated their lives to the children they served have also suffered similar undeserved fates. Entire nations have been gripped with fear after these events. This fear has, often, resulted in massive expenditures of government funds and allocation of considerable resources as officials have attempted to respond to the needs of their citizens. In the United States, Israel and Russia, the responses to a few of these terrible incidents were at least partially flawed. As one of the goals of terrorists is to cause governments to react ineffectively in what are often terrorist-created no-win situations, such flawed responses unwittingly contributed to the terrorists' success. Unfortunately, the focus sometimes shifts from coping with the emergency, treating the victims, and bringing those who commit atrocities to justice instead to criticism of government officials. And while government officials must be held accountable to those they serve, the public must understand that some acts of terrorism may take place no matter how effective the antiterrorism efforts of any nation. Nowhere is this truer than in a democracy where our unique and cherished freedoms sometimes make us vulnerable to those who intend to harm us.

Unfortunately, terrorists have scored what they see as successes in a number of these bloody attacks and we have naturally reacted as they desired – with fear and terror. These successes contribute to the likelihood of future incidents of terrorists targeting schools and children in both the U.S. and worldwide.

The time has come for a frank and insightful analysis of school terrorism incidents, for terrorism has grown to become a worldwide phenomenon. There are a wide variety of terrorists groups who have and may choose to, in the future, target school children in their efforts to sow fear. This book shall attempt to provide a direct appraisal of this crucial issue in clear terms as well as give much needed insight into potential solutions to this grave threat.

The authors began conducting intensive research into the topic in late 2002 to enhance their school and school bus terrorism presentations. After the tragic Beslan attack and announcements that American school floor plans had been recovered in Iraq, the authors were moved to make a contribution to the solution to this recent threat. At the same time, many people in the country were reacting to a media stir about the possibility of terrorist attacks on polling sites located in schools. While this type of attack, like hundreds of other scenarios, is certainly possible, these concerns have developed absent of any intelligence information and unfortunately resulted in a tremendous waste of time for school officials who were reacting to advice by those with no actual experience in the field of antiterrorism. While we are saddened that there is even a need for this book, we feel that these situations demonstrate that the need is significant. These events emphasize the need for a rational and calm assessment of the issue of school related terrorism. The presence of considerable disinformation, speculation and even reckless predictions concerning terrorism have negatively impacted public and private schools across the nation. When school boards across the country begin debating whether they should cease to allow their schools to be used as polling sites based on speculation, there is clearly a need for more accurate information.

As we shall see, there are those who have inadvertently helped to further the goals of terrorists with rhetoric and hype either through well meaning ignorance or the selfish desire to exploit the situation to line their own pockets. We will provide numerous examples of how unscrupulous consultants have done considerable damage by issuing reckless statements to the media, at conference presentations and providing false or inaccurate information through consulting work. Often such consultants lack qualifications either through actual experience or by formal training in an appropriate antiterrorism field.

We hasten to point out that during the extensive research of terrorism incidents for this book we found far more instances where targets other than schools, school buses and school children were attacked. As we have seen in the Beslan massacre, terrorists typically run considerable risks to, in the long term, harm of their goals if they select school children as targets. While it may be clear to readers that school related targets have and, likely, will again be selected, we wish to emphasize that the chances of any one school, bus or group of students being targeted are remote even in a nation like Israel where many of these types of attacks have occurred.

We shall also explore the dramatic impact of school terrorism incidents on the political landscape. Terrorism has placed a heavy burden on elected officials and taxed the resources, flexibility and patience of countless government officials with antiterrorism responsibilities. Educators, government school safety centers, the military, law enforcement, mental health, emergency management, public health, fire services, emergency medical services and other personnel have all been severely taxed in their efforts to make our schools a safe haven from terrorists who will stop at nothing to further their cause.

As a vivid example of the effort that those who protect children will expend, co-author Michael Dorn observed armed soldiers protecting school children on field trips at historical sites, museums and other locales while in Israel for antiterrorism training. When asked why men with automatic weapons always seemed to be near school children, ranking Israeli police officials told him that this measure was mandated after two separate attacks where terrorists gunned down Israeli children on field trips. The practice of soldiers accompanying all school children in the State of Israel has shown success on at least one occasion. Soldiers thwarted an attack by terrorists who tried to use a vehicle bomb to attack a school bus.

Though the soldiers gave their own lives in the process, they succeeded in protecting the children from harm.

An important part of any safe schools plan is getting the opinions of representatives of fields that are involved. The authors have, to this end, called on several national experts to lend their knowledge. Best selling author and expert on youth violence Lt. Col. Dave Grossman is a popular speaker at law enforcement and education conferences. He is considered one of the foremost experts on killing. Col. Grossman's books *On Killing* and *Stop Teaching Our Kids to Kill: A Call to Action Against T.V. and Video Game Violence* have shaped current thought on why, how and when people kill. Col. Grossman told the authors that in World War II more than 500,000 screened and selected American soldiers were not mentally able to do what they needed to because of the trauma of combat. He points out that if a trained and screened soldier can react in this manner, an incident like the Beslan attack could naturally have a significant impact on the emotional well – being of children who survive an attack.

Gregory Thomas knows first hand how a major terrorism event can impact school children when their school happens to be located in proximity to a terrorist target. Gregory served as the Executive Director for the Office of School Safety and Planning for the New York City Department of Education during both terrorist attacks on the World Trade Center. He now serves as the Director of the Program for School Preparedness at Columbia University. Gregory is one of a handful of people in the United States who has full time experience as a school safety practitioner and actual experience in response to a terrorism event impacting schools. Thomas emphasizes that school officials must prepare for terrorism not because of the motive behind the act, but because of the impact of the event. He, like the other experts we interviewed, stressed the need for schools and communities to follow the all – hazards approach to safe school planning as outlined by the United States Department of Education.

As the Director of School Safety and Security for Montgomery County, Maryland, Public Schools, Ed Clarke has also had to address the needs of his community due to acts of terrorism. His community was impacted by the shooting of a student at a school in a nearby community. Though the suspects were later apprehended and convicted on terrorism statutes, the period of time immediately following this attack left many students, parents and school employees feeling extremely vulnerable. Director Clarke tells attendees in his U.S. Department of Education training sessions that school and public safety officials need to plan together before a crisis such as an act of terrorism occurs. His experience was that these relationships in his community were invaluable during these trying times.

Ada Dolch was the principal of a magnet school located in close proximity to Ground Zero. She also lost a sister who worked in one of the towers in the attack. Ada Dolch has been credited with an amazingly well coordinated evacuation of her school during this most challenging crisis. Extensively practicing her building's evacuation procedures and planning in advance to use, if necessary, alternate forms of communications paid off on this fateful day. She emphasizes the need for constant communications and practice of emergency procedures with staff members and students, pointing out that a plan that simply sits on a shelf has little value during a crisis.

Of course, we are all concerned about the tremendous negative impact on the mental health of our children. And as the events of September 11, 2001 have shown us, a child need not witness an act of terrorism first hand to be impacted emotionally in significant ways according to Marleen Wong, one of the world's most widely recognized experts on crisis response and recovery for youth. As Director of the School Crisis and Intervention Unit for the National Center for Child Traumatic Stress at UCLA and Duke Universities and the Director of Crisis Counseling and Intervention Services for the Los Angeles Unified School District, Wong has worked extensively with children following such devastating incidents as the Murrah Building bombing in Oklahoma City, the Columbine High School shooting and bombing attack, and the second World Trade Center attack. She is another member of the short list of individuals with actual experience in dealing with terrorism and as a school safety practitioner. Ms. Wong points out that major crisis situations, such as an act of terrorism that impacts a school, can have a devastating effect on our children. She encourages school and community mental health officials to develop advanced recovery plans and capabilities to address any type of crisis incident that could occur.

Other top experts interviewed for this book also expressed concerns over the effect that terrorism is having on our youth and the schools where they are educated. Throughout this book, we shall draw on the experience of a number of top terrorism and antiterrorism experts while considering a number of particularly significant issues pertaining to terrorism and schools.

Readers should note that this book will not rely on the Federal Bureau of Investigation's standard definition of terrorism. In the book *Jane's Counter Terrorism,* author Christopher Kozlow points out that there are more than 100 official definitions for terrorism around the globe. As these definitions vary widely, and we are examining school related terrorism from a global perspective, we will consider incidents that fit many formal government definitions of terrorism and more importantly, fit the definition of terrorism for the man or woman on the street. After all, terrorism involves terrorizing the populace through specific acts rather than an academic classification of events meeting a rigid criteria. As our purpose is to inform rather than to reinforce any one government's definition of terrorism, we shall take a much broader view of the topic. This is not to indicate in any way that the definitions of agencies like the FBI are not valid. It is clear that such definitions are needed. Instead, we have taken this approach since there is a great deal of difference in how acts of terrorism are defined by the many countries where these acts have occurred, and we feel that these events may have implications for American schools. We trust most readers will see that the school terrorism incidents we discuss will fit many, if not most, definitions of terrorism around the world. Even when using this more inclusive approach to evaluating school related terrorism, we found these types of incidents to be extremely rare occurrences. However, inappropriate responses to some incidents have been extremely damaging and may have paved the way for more attacks.

We will also examine what schools should be doing to try to prevent acts of terrorism and prepare to respond to those acts that cannot be prevented. These topics will be examined in a fairly general way from the standpoint of best practices under the relatively new United States Department of Education and Jane's models for safe school planning. Since very few school systems and even fewer (if any) private schools have written safe schools plans that meet these suggested standards, this section is designed to help parents objectively evaluate their child's school while providing a condensed framework for educators who wish to ensure that their efforts are in accordance with recommended best practices.

We shall carefully explore some of the more likely scenarios for future incidents of school terrorism along with those that are far less likely but which could prove to be extremely deadly and/or disruptive. Hopefully, this book will also shatter some of the myths created by the numerous self proclaimed experts out there who in reality have no formal academic, experiential or training background in antiterrorism.

We will attempt to provide information on antiterrorism techniques and safe school planning considerations that are suitable for discussion in a public forum such as this book. We intentionally avoided some techniques and discussion of certain scenarios as we have no desire to further the aims of any terrorist who might read this book in their research. We also do not name school districts when we highlight their antiterrorism efforts if we feel that it could undermine their efforts in making such measures public.

We will also examine the critical issue of the emotional well being of our children following an attack. Relying on two of the world's top experts on recovery efforts for incidents of school terrorism, we shall provide a basic outline for the development of an effective, comprehensive and well written recovery plan as recommended by the U.S. Department of Education.

We will also provide a list of resources for the reader who wishes to learn more about these issues. As we do so throughout the book, we will focus our efforts on drawing attention to the numerous free governmental resources that are available to school officials.

We applaud readers for their acknowledgement that antiterrorism efforts for schools are necessary in today's world and are hopeful that this book will afford them some assistance in their efforts.

Terrorist Events

Chapter 1

History of
School Terrorism Incidents

From day care centers to our nation's largest universities, all campuses have the potential to be targeted by terrorists. Incidents where terrorist acts have impacted American schools as incidental targets include both World Trade Center attacks and the bombing of the Murrah Building in Oklahoma City. In another well known example, terrorism charges and conviction were obtained following the beltway sniper attacks which included the shooting on school property of a middle school student. This series of incidents had a dramatic impact on schools and pupil transportation in the Washington D.C. metro region. In July, 2004, police conducted a raid on an apartment rented by several terrorists involved in the Madrid train bombings that killed 191 people. Documents found in the apartment show that the terrorists had considered attacking a school.

As another example of how difficult it can be to properly classify some incidents that may be considered acts of school related terrorism, we can look at the most devastating school violence episode in this nation's history. It occurred in Bath, Michigan on May 18, 1927 when an enraged school board member named Andrew Kehoe became upset at the local school board. He placed a large amount of dynamite in the basement of the Bath Consolidated School, killing thirty nine students and teachers and injuring dozens of others in the building. While rescue efforts where underway after the explosion, Kehoe set off another bomb in his pick up truck killing himself, the superintendent of schools, a student and

> "Incidents where terrorist acts have impacted American schools as incidental targets include both World Trade Center attacks and the Bombing of the Murrah Building in Oklahoma City."

two bystanders. Kehoe was angry because school taxes had been raised and he was about to lose his farm to foreclosure. If this incident occurred today, some might classify it as an act of terrorism due to the use of powerful explosives to blow up a government building, the use of a secondary explosive device during rescue attempts and because Kehoe was motivated at least in part to protest higher taxes. Most government definitions of terrorism, however, would not cover this tragic incident because Kehoe was not part of a larger movement or shared philosophy and apparently carried out the attack to vent his extreme anger rather than to affect any social change. Had Kehoe acted upon a philosophy or belief system common to militia groups as the attackers in the Cokeville, Wyoming school attack (discussed later in this chapter) apparently did, we would have been more inclined to count this incident as an act of school terrorism.

These and other incidents in the United States and abroad must be examined to understand the implications of school related terrorism for American schools.

THE IMPORTANCE OF HISTORICAL REVIEW

It may also be helpful to review some other incidents of terrorism around the world that have impacted childcare facilities and K -12 schools. These attacks clearly have implications for American schools, as terrorist incidents such as airline hijackings that occur in other parts of the world can, at times, be predictive to similar problems at home. It is important to note that our research uncovered a number of attacks on institutions of higher learning as well as those listed here for school children.

SOME OF THE SITUATIONS REVIEWED DO NOT FIT ALL DEFINITIONS OF TERRORISM

Furthermore, we will examine some situations that do not fit all of the more than one hundred official definitions of terrorism used by governments around the world. A number of these incidents, for example, do not fit the definition developed by the Federal Bureau of Investigation and in standard usage in the United States. Definitions of terrorism vary from country to country and even within the states or provinces of particular countries like the United States.

For example, the Israeli government considered a multiple-victim shooting by a Middle Eastern gunman at the El Al ticket counter in the Los Angeles International Airport to be an act of terrorism, while the Federal Bureau of Investigation did not. While this attack did not fit the FBI definition of terrorism, the attack did shut down the airport on a busy holiday, capture the media focus and strike terror into the hearts of Jews and anyone else who happened to be traveling that day. To the Israeli government, this attack was, beyond doubt, an act of terrorism. Because we will be examining incidents in a number of countries, the authors have selected not to be bound by any one governmental definition of terrorism while examining school related incidents. We shall leave it to the reader to discern whether the incidents described fit their own definitions of terrorism or not.

OFF-CAMPUS INCIDENTS

Several incidents listed here clearly did not take place on a campus, but involved an apparent intentional targeting of students traveling to or from school or, in one case, participating in a parade. While methods of student travel to and from school are sometimes different in other countries, the impact of acts of violence directed against students using mass transit or while walking in groups is still relevant to campus officials. Other incidents involve atrocities committed by guerilla forces such as Chechen Rebels during periods of upheaval but would fit with most definitions of acts of terrorism by their nature. Direct attention has been given to those acts of intense violence that appeared to specifically target school children for the furtherance of some political motive or to affect social change.

OTHER INCIDENTS

While our research was intensive and we made every effort to uncover every school related attack, it is likely that a number of instances which should be included here were missed. For example, after several years conducting interviews and internet research, one of the coauthors was reading a book titled *March or Die – France and the Foreign Legion* by Tony Gerahghty for leisure. In the book, he ran across an account of the French Foreign Legion being called in to help rescue a school bus filled with children who had been taken hostage at the border between Somalia and Djibouti in 1976. By contrast, there was not a single reference to this incident after more than one hundred hours of internet research and numerous interviews with experts. Furthermore, the incident has never been mentioned in any of the advanced antiterrorism training programs that the authors have attended.

The above illustrates the difficulty of identifying every event. In another example, the coauthors have spent considerable time trying to track down a reported hostage taking by two militia members in a small Southeastern private school in the United States. A police academy instructor showed a copy of a series of television news segments covering this incident during a class in the early 1980's. When approached by one of the coauthors, the instructor remembers showing the tape and the basics of the incidents, but he no longer has the tape and cannot recall the city and year when the attack occurred. Thus far, our efforts to track the event down and properly document it have been unsuccessful. Having seen the tape while attending the class many years ago, coauthor Michael Dorn knows an incident occurred, but without more tangible information it would not be appropriate to list it here.

Readers who are familiar with incidents of school related terrorism that are not listed in this chapter are encouraged to contact the authors so the incident(s) can be added to our list of incidents on our website and in future editions of this book and to our conference presentations.

LIST OF TERRORIST EVENTS

However, despite the inherent difficulty in both categorizing and tracking down all likely terrorist events effecting schools, the authors have compiled the following reference list of more than thirty separate terrorist events occurring in more than twelve countries and territories around the world. To the author's knowledge, the following represents the most comprehensive public record of school related terrorist events in existence.

- March 18, 1968 - Fatah terrorists in Israel set a land mine which later blew up a school bus, killing two children and injuring 28 others.

- May 8, 1970 - Palestinian terrorists attacked an Israeli School bus killing nine children and three adults. Nineteen others were also crippled for life. The terrorists apparently knew the bus schedule and planned their attack based on this knowledge.

- May, 1974 - Three Arab terrorists dressed as Israeli Defense Forces soldiers attacked a school in Ma'alot, Israel. They took hostages and killed twenty two school children along with several adults. Many of the casualties occurred when an elite unit of the Golani Brigade attempted a tactical response to rescue the hostages. This incident resulted in the formation of special tactical units within the Israel National Police.

- 1976 – French Foreign Legion troops and the French counterterrorism police unit GIGN executed a tactical assault to free twenty nine French children being held hostage in a school bus at the border of Djibouti and Somalia. One child and five terrorists were killed during the rescue operation.

- May, 1977 – A group of four Moluccan terrorists took more than 100 students and school employees hostage in an elementary school in Bovendsmille, Holland. After fourteen days of patient negotiations, Dutch Royal Marines performed a successful tactical rescue and captured all four terrorists.

- May, 1986 – In a bizarre incident, a man and his wife who both held extremist views and wished to create a "Brave New World" took students and teachers hostage at an elementary school in Cokeville, Wyoming using firearms and explosives. They shot a teacher in the back and accidentally detonated the device killing the wife and injuring some of the hostages.

- February, 1993 – Terrorists detonate a vehicle bomb in the parking deck of the World Trade Center in an attempt to collapse both towers. Six people were killed and more than a thousand injured in the attack. Schools in the immediate area were affected by the event, but no students or staff were injured

• May, 1994 – Four Chechens armed with grenades and firearms hijacked a bus filled with teachers, parents and children in Southern Russia. The hostages were released after a multi-million dollar ransom was paid.

• April, 1995 – Shortly after parents had dropped their children off at a day care center located in the Murrah Federal Building in Oklahoma City, a large car bomb detonated and destroyed half of the structure. Among the 168 people who were killed were children at the day care center. Area schools also suffered structural damage.

> "Shortly after parents had dropped their children off at a day care center located in the Murrah Federal Building in Oklahoma City, a large car bomb detonated and destroyed half of the structure. Among the 168 people who were killed were children at the day care center."
> Press Reports

• March, 1997 – Seven Israeli school girls were shot to death by a Jordanian soldier while on a field trip in Bakura, Jordan.

• January, 1998 – A bombing in Algiers on a crowded street packed with students returning home from school killed one person and wounded several others.

• March, 1998 – The American School in Amman, Jordan was rocked by an explosion believed to be the work of terrorists upset by the U.S. conflict with Iraq over U.N. arms inspections.

• October 29, 1998 - An Israeli soldier was killed after a terrorist drove a car bomb into an army jeep the soldier was driving. The jeep was escorting a bus of 40 elementary school children from Kfar Darom, a settlement in the Gaza strip.

• August, 1999 – An individual with extremist views opened fire in a childcare area of a Jewish community center in Los Angeles and killed several children. Police officers pursued the suspect who then shot and killed a Hispanic postal employee. The killings stemmed from the suspect's anti-Semitic and racist views.

• November, 2000 – A bomb targeting a school bus exploded in the Gaza Strip settlement of Kfar Darom killing two passengers and wounding twelve others, including five school children.

- April, 2001 – A car bomb targeting a school bus exploded near the town of Nablus in the West Bank. One Palestinian was killed and another injured.

- May 30, 2001 – A car bomb exploded outside a school in Netanya where students were studying for exams. Injuries were lessened by the time of the incident, which was after most people had gone home. Eight people were injured in the attack .

- September, 2001 – Two people died and three more were injured in a terrorist attack on a minibus loaded with school and kindergarten teachers near the Adam Junction in Israel.

- September, 2001 – A terrorist bomber's head rolled into a French-language school in Jerusalem as children were arriving to start their school day. The bomber, who was disguised as an Orthodox Jew, blew himself up and injured eleven people next to the school.

- September, 2001 – A bomb thrown at Catholic school girls walking to class through a Protestant neighborhood in Ireland exploded. Four police officers who were escorting the children were injured.

- November, 2001 – A Palestinian gunman killed two students and wounded more than forty other passengers when he attacked their bus with an M-16 rifle at a bus stop in Jerusalem. An armed bystander and members of the Israel Border Police stopped the attack when they killed the gunman.

- March, 2002 – A terrorist homicide bomber killed seven and wounded dozens more when he blew himself up on a bus frequently used by Arab and Jewish school children, many of whom were injured.

- March, 2002 – Five students were shot to death and twenty - three other people wounded in an attack by Palestinian terrorists on a pre-military high school in Atzmona, Israel.

- May, 2002 – Twelve school children were among the victims killed in Dagestan when a large remote-controlled explosive device detonated as they passed it. Russian President Vladimir Putin compared the terrorists who carried out the attack to the Nazis.

- June, 2002 – Two students were murdered and fifteen wounded by a gunman believed to be from an ethnic minority Karen rebel group in an attack on a school bus in Thailand.

- June 18, 2002 – A homicide bomber detonated himself on a bus headed towards Jersusalem. The bus, which was carrying many students on their way to school, was destroyed, leaving nineteen dead and seventy-four others wounded.

- August, 2002 – Three school employees and two school security personnel were killed by gunman in an attack on the Murree Christian School in Pakistan.

- September 5, 2002 – Fatah terrorists fired shots from a crowded school towards a patrol of Israeli soldiers. One soldier was killed and another wounded.

- October, 2002- During a series of sniper attacks in the Washington, D.C. area, the Beltway snipers killed ten people and wounded three others, causing significant panic in the region. On October, seventh, 2002, a thirteen year old boy was shot and wounded as he arrived at Benjamin Tasker Middle School in Bowie, Maryland. The shooting rampage ended when John Allen Muhammad and Lee Boyd Malvo were arrested and charged with some of the attacks. In March, 2004, Muhammad was sentenced to death after his conviction on terrorism statutes. Malvo was sentenced to life in prison.

- November, 21, 2002 – A terrorist bomber killed eleven people and injured almost fifty others in Israel when he blew himself up on a bus crowded with school children. The terrorist group Hamas claimed responsibility for the attack.

- April, 2003 – An explosion at a high school in Jennin, West Bank injured nearly thirty students. A radical Jewish group - Nikmat Olelim or "Revenge of the Infants" claimed responsibility for the incident saying the bomb was placed to avenge the murders of Jewish children by Palestinian terrorists.

- February 22, 2004 - A Fatah attack on a bus in Jerusalem killed eight and wounded sixty more. Eleven of those wounded were school children.

- June 28, 2004 – One adult and one child were killed when a rocket fired by Hamas terrorists in the Gaza strip detonated in a nursery school in Sderot.

- September, 2004 – An attack by Chechen terrorists on a school in Belsan, Russia leaves hundreds dead and appears to be the largest terrorist attack on a school related target to date.

- November 8, 2004 – A bomb went off damaging a Muslim elementary school in Eindhoven. No one was injured in the attack. Police feel that attack is related to a series of terrorist incidents in the region.

By looking at these and other violent acts perpetrated by extremists around the world, we may be better able to understand the vulnerabilities of our students and campuses here in America. Of particular note is the trend for targeting school and commuter buses transporting students. Fortunately, the United States Department of Education, the Federal Emergency Management Agency, the Bureau of Alcohol, Tobacco and Firearms, the United States Department of Homeland Security, the Transportation Security Administration and other state and federal agencies have been making efforts to address issues relating to terrorism impacting our campuses and school buses. Readers should also keep in mind that terrorists have selected a wide range of targets and that campuses and students historically represent a small portion of attacks on many other types of targets. While conducting the research for this book, we found far more attacks on other types of targets than on schools. Thus far, school related targets have not been the type of target favored by terrorists. As a final note, the fragmented, widely varied and proliferating sources of terrorism

"Of particular note is the trend for targeting school and commuter buses transporting students"

around the globe make it difficult to determine the kind and nature of attacks in the future.

Chapter 2

The Tragedy at Beslan

It was the first day of school at Middle School No. 1 in the remote city, and students and their parents had converged in the schoolyard for the traditional celebrations that accompanied the beginning of each school year. Students walked to class bearing flowers and small gifts for their teachers. Suddenly, a van and a large military truck arrived on the scene and from the back poured a mass of masked gunmen. The terrorists engaged police in a small gun battle, leaving one terrorist and five police dead. They next entered the schoolyard, ordering everyone inside. Many students thought at first that it was some sort of joke or drill, but when one of the terrorists shot a man for attempting to comfort others, they knew it was real.

The massacre at Beslan had begun.

Chaos engulfed the school as the gunmen herded more than one thousand children and adults into the gymnasium. The terrorists soon established a strict set of rules: those who protested or tried to escape would be shot. One man was killed as he stood up, another as he ran out through the back door towards freedom. Another man was told: "You, quiet the children, otherwise we'll shoot you!" A minute later, the children continued to cry, and the man was shot. The killers dragged the dead through the crowd to another room, leaving a trail of blood to remind everyone of the consequences of an incorrect action. They gave the authorities similar incentives for compliance – for every terrorist killed there would be 50 hostages executed, and 20 more for each terrorist wounded.

Next, like clockwork, they began to place a highly complex network of bombs throughout the gym and tripwires around the building. Eyewitnesses claim that the terrorists placed anywhere from 10 to 30 bombs throughout the mass of hostages, and that the work was completed within half an hour. When they finished, the hostages were told "one press of a button was enough to detonate everything." In addition to the stationary explosives, two female suicide bombers dressed in black running outfits patrolled the room, each carrying a pistol in one hand and a detonator in the other. There was no uncertainty as to the outcome of this situation. The terrorists had come to the school prepared to die.

> "Eyewitnesses claim that the terrorists placed anywhere from 10 to 30 bombs placed throughout the mass of hostages, and that the work was completed within half an hour."

Remembering the opiate gas used to knock out the Chechen hostage takers in a Moscow theater in 2002, the terrorists came prepared with gas masks. They instructed the hostages to hand in their cell phones, warning them: "If we hear somebody's telephone ringing, 20 people around you will be killed." The rules were strict, even for hostages being released. On the second day of the siege, 26 women and children were allowed to leave, but some mothers with more than one child were forced to choose only one to take with them. As the women were released, the terrorists set off two rocket-powered grenades around the school to dissuade authorities from any attempted rescue.

While they joked with the hostages about being 'such kind terrorists,' the brutality of the hostage-takers was unquestionable. Some terrorists were even killed by the leader of the group for objecting to kill children.

The hostage-takers requested and received the same negotiator that successfully negotiated the release of children in the Moscow Theater siege. The talks failed, however, and food, water and medicines were not allowed into the school. With water supplies running low, the buckets used to distribute water were replaced by clothes soaked in water and thrown to the group. One terrorist told a hostage that Russian forces had poisoned the water and that one terrorist had already succumbed from drinking it. As the hours wore on, the one-at-a-time bathroom policy disappeared and children began relieving themselves in the crowd. After endless hours in captivity, some were in such pain from thirst that they drank urine that they collected in rolled up clothes and even shoes.

By this point, a mob had gathered outside the school. In addition to Russian police, security, and Special Forces, there were hundreds of armed and angry fathers of the hostages. The vigilante mob was so distrustful of the integrity and competence of the government that they blocked some of the military forces from getting near the area.

On the third day of the conflict, both sides reached an agreement for rescue workers to remove some of the bodies from the gym. Reports of what happened next vary. Some reports blame a loose bomb falling and detonating, others blame a terrorist accidentally setting off a trip wire, and still more believe that the workers sent in to remove bodies attempted a rescue. Most of the evidence seems to point at the angry mob for firing the first shots, initiating a gun battle with the terrorists, who then set off all of the bombs. Whatever the cause, what happened next would be the gory end to what newspapers called "52 Hours of Fear"

> "However many escapees there actually were, it is clear that the perimeter established by police had failed to keep anyone in or out of the school."

At 1:04 p.m. one bomb went off, then another. Witnesses say that those unlucky enough to be seated near the bombs absorbed most of the blasts, so those further away escaped harm initially. After the explosions, a desperate scramble for freedom ensued, with people pouring through doors and out windows in any direction available. The remaining terrorists began shooting and killing hostages as they fled. A struggle ensued between a mix of terrorists, soldiers, police and the vigilante mob. The military attacked the school with brute force, using helicopter gun ships and at least one tank.

Russian forces finally took the school at 3 p.m., except for a group of three gunmen in the basement who still held hostages. The terrorists and the hostages were all killed. Outside of the school, 13 hostage-takers escaped, two of them blending in with the crowd disguised as health personnel. More were cornered in a two-story house near the school, and the location was destroyed around 11 p.m. by tanks and flamethrowers. However many escapees there actually were, it is clear that the perimeter established by police had failed to keep anyone in or out of the school.

No one really knows how many died at Beslan, and it is unclear if anyone ever will. "Official" estimates range anywhere from 330 to more than 400 dead, and some believe that the number is actually three times higher. It is doubtful, considering the state of Russian affairs, whether or not a more accurate number will be reached.

BACKGROUND

The hundreds of parents and children in the school were caught up in the middle of nearly two centuries of fighting between Russia and Chechnya. Chechnya, along with neighboring Dagestan, is an Islamic state that was engulfed by the then strongly Orthodox Catholic Russia during its period of imperialist expansion. Since being swallowed by Russia in the 19th century, Chechnya has been embroiled in rebellion and war, evolving recently into a guerilla war fought with ties to Arab jihadists, using the tactics of international terrorists to aid their fight for freedom.

In 1944 towards the end of World War II, Stalin deported ethnic Chechens to Siberia as punishment for alleged Nazi collaboration. More than 10 years later, they were allowed to return, where they remained under authoritarian Soviet rule. Then, in the 1990s, Chechnya took advantage of the fall of the Soviet Union and declared independence. This rebellion was halted within a few years when Russian troops invaded, setting off a war that would result in the deaths of more than 100,000 Chechens, many of them children.

Because of the bloody war, many Chechen rebels have moved on to dirtier means to ensure their voice will be heard. Though direct ties are tenuous, there remains no doubt that the rebels at least share an ideology of terror with Al-Qaeda. Russian authorities received an email from Shamil Basayev, a leading Chechen radical and known mercenary who claimed responsibility for the attack, on September 17th. The email confirms this ideology, and justifies the September 1st attack in Beslan:

"We regret what happened in Beslan. It's simply that the war, which Putin declared on us five years ago, has destroyed more than 40,000 Chechen children and crippled more than 5,000 of them, has gone back to where it started from."

Basayev also claimed responsibility for a string of recent terrorist attacks that have left more than 430 dead, including a bus stop bombing near Moscow, a Moscow subway homicide bombing, and a coordinated attack that downed two passenger planes simultaneously in August. Apart from these recent attacks, there have also been at least two other school-related attacks in the region that can be attributed to the Chechen-Russian conflict (these are detailed in Chapter 1).

COMPLICATIONS OF FREEDOM

The email also beseeched Russian President and noted hard-liner Vladimir Putin to withdraw troops from Chechnya and recognize its independence. In return for this concession, Basayev promised to cut all ties to armed struggle against Russia and anti-Russian activities.

In an interview, Dr. Adam Stulberg of the Sam Nunn School of International Affairs at the Georgia Institute of Technology said that the demands given by the terrorists at Beslan are more reasonable than those in the Moscow theater siege in 2002. However, this seems to be more a result of a Chechen rebel learning curve and not a sign of moderation on the part of the terrorists. Anatol Lieven of the Carnegie Endowment for International Peace has said that further ethnic conflict "is undoubtedly what these terrorists hope to provoke."

Given that assessment of the situation, it is not surprising that Putin has refused to give any ground in the conflict. When world leaders, including President Bush, have called his hard-line stance toward Chechen terrorism into question, Putin cites the pandering of Hitler in the 1930s. Any concessions, he claims, will result in a widening of demands and growth in violence, as the world saw when Hitler was appeased with the Sudetenland before World War II.

One positive result of the horror of this attack is the reaction by not only Russians and the rest of the world but of Chechens and Muslims. One newspaper responded with an article penned by a disgusted Muslim: 'Our terrorist sons are the end product of our corrupted culture.' Immediately after the incident, Chechen separatist leaders condemned the attack and denied any ties or involvement to the perpetrators. Hopefully this common abhorrence will lead to a further reduction of support for the rebels in Chechnya, as was seen in Ireland in the 1990's.

Putin's hard line stance and assertion that the attack was the result of "Russia's weakness" has resulted in relatively little negative impact to his popularity among the Russian populace. What can be considered a 'nose-dive' in his ratings was actually a drop from 80% support before the attack to 60% afterwards. Another poll showed that 54% of those surveyed felt that police and security forces were corrupt and to blame for allowing the attack. In addition, post-attack "anti-terrorism" rallies in Russia seem to be more of a show of support for Putin than one of sympathy for the victims of the attacks.

> "Terrorists can be capable of killing children due to a number of dynamics. Group dynamics as we saw with the Nazis executing Jewish children were observed when those that protested were killed. In the Beslan incident, one of the terrorists was reportedly shot after refusing to kill children. Another factor is the dehumanization of society to violence."
> Lt. Col. Dave Grossman

Putin's response to the situation has been a stronger authoritarian government – voters have lost some of their direct voice, governmental power has been further centralized, the death penalty has been reinstated, and the Soviet relic of encouraging citizens to spy on each other has returned. Surprisingly, a backlash of violence in the region has not occurred, except for a few isolated incidents. In one, fathers of the hostages beat a suspected hostage-taker to death after he was taken to the hospital. In another, police beat an aide to a member of the Duma (the Russian Parliament) from Dagestan after they heard his Chechen-sounding last name.

Overall, the region surrounding Chechnya is not very supportive of their cause. While there are strong religious and ethnic ties in the region, most (including many Chechens) are so afraid — and rightly so — of Russian reprisals that they remain uninvolved. In addition, there is a popular perception among Russians of Chechens as mountain savages with no culture or morals, and repeated Chechen terrorist attacks in the heart of Moscow only serve to turn this perception into a feeling of hate and distrust.

WORLDWIDE IMPLICATIONS

The effects of the recent violence are being felt worldwide. Former New York City mayor Rudolph Giuliani expressed support for Putin, comparing the Beslan massacre to the United States' September 11th. In Hudson, Massachusetts, parents were fearful of similar attacks in the U.S., worried that the location of polling places in school buildings would attract violence. They demanded that elections not be held in schools, and school officials responded by stating that students gain a necessary benefit from seeing elections take place firsthand.

The importance of holding fast with plans and continuing everyday life, as with the example of elections, is discussed elsewhere in this book (chapters 3, 4, and 10). Changing plans in response to terrorist acts, or otherwise living in fear, only demonstrates to terrorists that their acts are having an ongoing impact. On the contrary, resolutely moving forward following a terrorist attack demonstrates the ineffectiveness of their violent acts on the rest of society.

LESSONS LEARNED

The biggest lesson to be taken from this tragedy is that of the complete failure to prevent the attack in any way or to mitigate the situation once it started. Most agree that the supplies used by the terrorists were hidden in the school months before. One report claims that a Chechen construction company was doing work in the school during July of 2004, and this is believed to be the gap exploited by the rebels. While current conditions in Russia are very different from those in the U.S., this issue applies to the safety of American schools. Careful attention to who is doing work on your school or employed around your students can not only help prevent acts like that in Beslan, but also curb theft of school property, embezzlement, and child abductions and molestation. These crimes and others have repeatedly been found to be a result of poor screening of job applicants for the school environment.

Another blaring mistake was the failure of the perimeter around the school. The faulty cordon made it possible for the vigilante mob of parents to storm further inside the school than Russian security forces, preventing them from doing their jobs. Parents were allowed to go inside and visit their children after the attack, many of them armed. This created a state of chaos and confusion, and gave some of the terrorists an easy route of escape. The importance of establishing a secure perimeter as well as utilizing a family reunification center could not have been shown any more clearly than in Beslan.

Note: This chapter was written within a few months of the attack, and all information was gathered from news reports and interviews with experts from around the world. The situation in Russia and Chechnya will no doubt continue to change. For these reasons, the information contained in this chapter is subject to alteration or may be retracted.

Chapter 3

The Miracle of Bovendsmilde

On a typical Monday morning in May of 1977 a group of four Moluccan terrorists armed with submachine guns and hand grenades burst into an elementary school in Bovendsmilde, Holland and took 105 students, the school's principal and several teachers hostage. At about the same time, another group of nine Moluccan terrorists hijacked a train just outside of town, taking 60 people hostage.

This difficult situation posed significant challenges for educators, police and military officials who were tasked with successfully resolving the situation, which escalated rapidly. At one point, terrorists in the school announced that they were becoming impatient with police and were preparing to throw hand grenades into the group of children. It was at this point that the principal and teachers quietly agreed among themselves that they could not allow this to happen. They made a pact that if the terrorists threw the grenades, the closest educator to each grenade would throw themselves on it to protect the children. No educator should ever have to make such a noble but horrific decision. Fortunately, hostage negotiators were able to calm the terrorists down and they did not carry out this plan.

As the situation progressed, the terrorists made impossible demands on the Dutch government and proved to be very difficult to deal with. Police negotiators did, however, have some success in gaining the freedom of at least a few of the children. One girl was released as a goodwill gesture

"As the situation progressed, the terrorists made impossible demands on the Dutch government and proved to be very difficult to deal with."

the terrorists. As the crisis dragged on, another significant problem arose to compound the crisis. A number of the children became violently ill. When a doctor spoke with one of the terrorists, the information he was given made him suspect that meningitis might be spreading among the children. The terrorists were not prepared for this type of problem and began to panic. Police negotiators were finally able to convince the terrorists to release the children who were in the most serious conditions. After their release, the children recovered and meningitis was ruled out as the cause.

After two weeks of patient negotiations, the terrorists became extremely difficult to deal with. Police became very concerned that the terrorists were likely to execute a number of their hostages in both locations. A carefully planned and extremely well executed tactical assault was carried out simultaneously on both locations.

First, fighter jets were used to create a diversion for the terrorists on the train. As they flew a mere 100 feet above the train, the pilots hit their afterburners, causing a deafening noise. Using thermal imaging equipment and other technology to gather intelligence, Royal Dutch Marines had determined the location of each terrorist on the train. Marines accurately predicted that the noise from the jets would cause the hostages to dive for cover and stop moving for a brief period of time. At this time the Marines fired into the compartments they knew contained terrorists, killing six of the nine terrorists.

In a classic tactical operation, three teams of commandos stormed the train simultaneously using explosives to blast open the doors of the train. During the resulting gunfight, three terrorists were captured. Unfortunately, two hostages were killed in the complex and difficult operation. Amazingly, only two of the marines were seriously wounded and none were killed.

Royal Dutch Marines carried out another daring and precise tactical operation at the elementary school. Marines drove an armored vehicle through a wall of the school to gain entry. Using thermal imaging and other equipment, the marines knew where they could breach the wall without harming the hostages. With blinding speed, the marines

> "Marines accurately predicted that the noise from the jets would cause the hostages to dive for cover and stop moving for a brief period of time. At this time the Marines fired into the compartments they knew contained terrorists, killing six of the nine terrorists."

captured all of the terrorists without a shot fired and without injury to any of the hostages.

AN EXAMPLE OF A SUCCESSFUL COUNTER-TERRORISM OPERATION

The manner in which this difficult and potentially volatile situation was resolved is still used today as an example of how a tactical response by highly trained, well led and properly equipped counterterrorism personnel can, when necessary, be used to save hostages when all other measures fail. The use of daring but thoroughly rehearsed tactics combined with application of what, at the time, was the latest available technology, helped make this difficult mission possible.

While a tactical response is not the most desirable way to end a hostage situation, it is sometimes necessary. The handling of this situation by Dutch authorities and counterterrorism personnel is used as an example of a nearly textbook application of patient negotiations combined with a proper tactical response when negotiations failed. The calm and admirable manner of the four educators who were held hostage clearly helped make it possible for commandos to execute a successful rescue. This case also demonstrates the importance of close collaboration between school and public safety officials before an incident. In addition, the job of the Royal Dutch Marines would have been less difficult if they had access to a number of current-day preplanning tools such as a virtual tour of the school. Miracles like those at an elementary school in Bovendsmilde do not just happen. They occur because officials and response personnel do not wait for tragedy to strike to plan and prepare for the incidents they pray will never happen.

> "Using thermal imaging and other equipment, the marines knew where they could breach the wall without harming the hostages. With blinding speed, the marines captured all of the terrorists without a shot being fired and without injury to any of the hostages."

Chapter 4

Terrorism and
Turkish Schools

The methodical and even institutional targeting of schools, students and teachers in Turkey by the ruthless terrorist group PKK – The Worker's Party of Kurdistan, was so pervasive and occurred on so many occasions, that we felt the situation should be addressed in its own chapter. During our research, we found numerous scattered news stories, government documents and other sources of information which present a somewhat disjointed and incomplete picture of the tragedies resulting from the direct targeting of not only the innocent children and teachers, but the very institution of education in the republic.

According to the Ministry of Foreign Affairs for the Republic of Turkey, from 1984 to 1994, 217 school teachers were abducted and murdered by the PKK in Southeastern Turkey. It is of particular note that the majority of teachers who were murdered were primary school educators. With many of the victims paying for their dedication to education of Turkey's children by being summarily shot or hanged, these brutal murders were one facet of a campaign by the PKK to virtually shut down Turkey's educational system. While other key parts of Turkish critical infrastructure were likewise targeted during this period, the attacks on schools, children and teachers were a particularly painful burden for the nation to bear. The wholesale slaughter of students and teachers by the PKK is gruesome to a different level because the attacks were frequent and pervasive over an extended period. It would be impossible to accurately quantify the emotional impact of these attacks on students, teachers and parents.

As we have seen with the beheadings of numerous hostages kidnapped by terrorists in Iraq, the repeated murders of innocent school teachers was clearly designed to generate considerable fear among teachers and at least in part, to dissuade them from continuing their work. Attacking schools by attempting to destroy them with fire created an entirely different problem for the Turkish government to try to address. Utilization of these two different types of violence increased the drain on available government resources while creating a tremendous amount of fear in the region.

Of course, these were not the only types of school related attacks carried out by the PKK. The deaths of four school children in November of 2003 in Sirnak is one example. A group of children found and began to play with a metal object near their school. The object was an explosive device placed there by members of the PKK.

According to the Ministry of Foreign Affairs, by the end of 1993 roughly 700 schools were closed due to the murders of teachers and hundreds of school arsons carried out by the PKK. In the end, approximately 3,600 schools had to be closed, denying a proper education to more than 100,000 school children. The scale of targeting school related personnel and buildings by the PKK appears to be unprecedented at least from the results of our research on the topic. Likewise, the impact of the attacks caused a massive and devastating impact upon the republic and necessitated a resource draining response from the Turkish government. The Turkish government estimates that it had to spend roughly 10 billion dollars per year just to combat the PKK.

Turkey is not alone in having its schools affected by internal strife. In Afghanistan in the 1990s the Taliban systematically took steps to reduce the number of schools and those who could attend them. It is estimated that some 1.5 million people have died in the country, many of these women, teachers, and children. Education is almost at a standstill, with literacy at a very low rate – 4% for women. Women had been banned from working or attending public schools, and in 1998 the Taliban closed more than one hundred privately funded schools that catered to women. This was a natural policy for a government which regularly detained, tortured and raped women that they felt were violating Islamic law.

The effects in Afghanistan are an extreme case study of what terrorism can do to a country. Today, 42% of those surveyed report suffering from Post Traumatic Stress Disorder (PTSD) and 97% suffer from major depression. The damaging effects on schools themselves incident by incident cannot compare to the other results of a government that left education and healthcare on the back burner to war and terrorism.

The PKK was established in 1974 as a part of a broader independence movement to try to force the Turkish government to establish a Kurdish state in Southeastern Turkey. The group's leader, Abdullah Ocalan, was a student at Ankara University. The group espoused Marxist beliefs and desired originally to create a communist revolution in Turkey. The group made a practice of targeting Kurds who supported or cooperated with the Turkish government. The PKK's activities occurred amidst the backdrop of a great deal of unrest and instability in Turkey. The Turkish National Security Council tallied more than 43,000 incidents of terrorism and an average of 28 deaths per day due to acts of terrorists between 1978 and 1982. These statistics are significant when we attempt to evaluate the implications of school related terrorism in regions with considerable instability and large numbers of disaffected people. Incidents of terrorism in regions like Southern Russia and Southeastern Turkey who were experiencing periods of civil unrest do have implications in other regions, but are unlikely to occur in the same manner and on the same level of frequency. For example, terrorists in other countries could decide to emulate a particular type of attack carried out under these conditions, but might not have the resources to carry out a series of attacks because of the relative small size of their group. Other differences must also be considered when evaluating these situations for their applicability in other countries.

For example, the tactical capabilities and very different approach utilized by the Dutch government in the elementary school attack in Bovendsmilde or tactical abilities and

> "In World War II, we had over 500,000 screened and selected GI's who were not mentally able to do what needed to be done because of the trauma of combat. If a screened and trained soldier can react like that, what kind of effect does an event like Beslan have on children?"
> Lt. Col. Dave Grossman

practices of law enforcement agencies in the United States highly contrast the manner in which the Russian government approached the Beslan incident. Even the post incident responses may be different. For example, it is hard to imagine parents being asked to view the bodies of hundreds of murdered children lying on the ground covered with raincoats and newspapers in order to see if their child is among the dead. The images of blood covered teddy bears in the school being broadcast on television would also be unlikely in the United States or many other countries such as Canada, England or Germany where crime scene control is typically more efficient. Mental health recovery capabilities in the United States are also more advanced than we might see in a nation with significant government instability where a higher percentage of available funding must be directed to security efforts. As he points out in his presentations, Lt. Colonel Dave Grossman feels that our responses to incidents similar to those that occur in other countries may need to be different than those taken to date. The United States is very different from most other nations and has a range of cultural, legal and ethical standards that often come into play when addressing terrorism concerns. These standards necessitate different responses than those that might be used and even used effectively in other countries.

The school related attacks in Israel, Turkey, Russia and other far away places do have implications for those responsible for safe school plan development and emergency response officials. Reviewing the incidents that have taken place elsewhere can be a useful way to consider whether local school safety plans are adequate. Every school system and private school in our country should have an emergency operations plan that is well developed enough to address a situation like the one in Beslan. This is true not only because a violent act of that scale could occur here, but more so because schools must be prepared to address other types of mass casualty incidents such as those that could result from an earthquake or aircraft disaster impacting a school.

As we shall see in later chapters, application of the best practices established by the United States Department of Education and Jane's models for safe school planning are prudent efforts that should be in use in all schools. When properly applied, these models will prepare schools and communities to better handle situations even of the horrendous scale of the incident in Beslan. While some with the responsibility to establish proper safe school plans are still in denial, it is imperative that we recognize that any school can be the scene of a disaster. Failure to develop a proper safe school plan under the new models is not only a serious oversight, but an inexcusable failure to properly safeguard our children in today's world.

Terrorist Tendencies

Chapter 5

Why Terrorists Target School Children

For the normal, well adjusted individual, the idea of intentionally harming a child is repulsive. Why then, would a terrorist or a group of terrorists intentionally select a school, school bus, school event or a group of school children in the community as a target for an act of violence?

TERRORIST TARGETING OF SCHOOLS IS A RARE EVENT

There are a variety of reasons that terrorists do on occasion select school children and staff as targets. Fortunately, there are also reasons that sometimes prevent terrorists from targeting school children as well. These reasons may help to explain perhaps why, thus far, terrorists have only targeted school children on rare occasions. Terrorists target schools because they are relatively soft targets and powerful symbolic targets. Schools and school functions can also provide opportunities for terrorists to create a mass casualty event with large numbers of young children as victims. Attacks on innocent children evoke a strong emotional reaction and draw intensive media coverage

ATTACKS ON CHILDREN CAN CAUSE SEVERE RESPONSE

Terrorists sometimes realize that an attack on school children can hurt the objectives of their organization. Terrorist groups that victimize children run the risk of alienating those people, organizations and governments that sometimes offer them support. Many (almost all) terrorist organizations have received fiscal support, hiding places, weapons

> "There are a variety of reasons that terrorists do on occasion select school children and staff as targets. Fortunately, there are also reasons that sometimes prevent terrorists from targeting school children as well."

61

and other forms of support from outside their organization. In these instances, terrorists must consider the concerns of those who support them or risk losing that support. An attack on children, depending on the sensibilities of those who provide assistance, can cost terrorists the support they desperately need to operate.

Another consideration for terrorists who contemplate a school related attack can be the severity of the governmental response to this type of attack. Targeting school children can have the affect of drawing a much more pronounced response in terms of antiterrorism and counterterrorism efforts. Terrorists may fear that an attack on school children could result in a more concerted effort by governments against their organization. This type of attack can also destroy sympathy for their cause among the world community, particularly in the country where the attack occurs. As terrorists are often focused on the image they create through their acts, this type of reaction can again be counterproductive if they are trying to affect public opinion through their efforts.

The terrorists may thus find themselves in the difficult position of having to weigh the significant impact of an act of school terrorism against the damage that may befall their cause should they go too far in their efforts to terrorize. While there have been instances where terrorist attacks have been poorly planned and badly executed with little thought given to logistics or the actual impact that the attack would have on society, other instances demonstrate a great deal of planning and thought prior to the actual attack. The September 11, 2001 attacks are a prime example of a carefully planned and executed terrorist attack. In this same attack, we see an example of a situation where some experts feel that the planners may have underestimated the response such a massive attack would generate. The aggressive response by the United States to this attack could also cause terrorists groups to consider very carefully what the response would be to a major attack on an American school.

THE EFFECTS OF MAJOR GOVERNMENT RESPONSE

There have been a number of instances where an aggressive governmental response has all but neutralized a previously powerful terrorist group following an act of terrorism that shocked the consciousness of the public. For example, aggressive action on the part of the Basque separatist group – ETA to target security personnel resulted in a massive effort on the part of the Spanish government. In December of 1997, this effort resulted in all 23 leaders of the group's political wing – Herri Batasuna, being captured by Spanish security forces. This action, followed by the tightening of international anti-terrorist efforts in the wake of 9/11, has seriously effected ETA's ability to function as a terrorist organization.

TERRORIST MOTIVATIONS TO ATTACK SCHOOLS

When terrorists do decide to attack school children, they may have one or more of the following motivations:

Schools and school buses are relatively soft targets that can be challenging to protect against acts of terrorism. Schools typically do not have the level of physical security of many other potential targets such as airports, government buildings and military installations. Elementary schools and school buses are particularly vulnerable and a review of past incidents indicates that they are also targeted more frequently than other types of school related targets.

Schools and school children are powerful symbolic targets. The average person feels a close connection to young people. Whether they are children, grandchildren, nieces, nephews or the neighbors' children, most people feel some connection to children. By targeting school children, terrorists can make people feel an inability to protect the children in their life. Since the targeting of school children is such an emotional issue, it is also very effective from a symbolic standpoint. When terrorists desire to show the inability of the government to protect the public from terrorist acts, the victimization of school children can be a powerful example.

As evidenced by the Beslan attack, schools can also provide terrorists with a potential for mass casualties with large numbers of children as victims. With attacks like the Murrah Building bombing in Oklahoma City, and both attacks on the World Trade Center, there seems to be an increased desire on the part of at least some terrorist organizations to move towards events that are likely to cause mass casual-

"There have been a number of instances where an aggressive governmental response has all but neutralized a previously powerful terrorist group following an act of terrorism that shocked the consciousness of the public."

ties. The Beslan attack involved hundreds of victims, many of them children, which clearly added to the efforts of the terrorists to create devastation with a single attack. Other types of attacks on schools could create mass casualty events including those utilizing powerful explosives and chemicals. Some special events associated with schools, such as graduation ceremonies and athletic events, draw large numbers of people and could be selected for a mass casualty effect. This type of attack is one more reason why school emergency preparedness measures must address mass casualty incidents. While other types of disasters can cause a mass casualty incident at a school, certain terrorism scenarios (such as a chemical attack) would pose many difficulties for communities without a proper four phase all hazards plan as described in this book.

"Attacks on innocent children evoke a strong emotional reaction."

Attacks on innocent children evoke a strong emotional reaction. We often react with even greater horror when we observe victims of a terrorist attack on the news when they are children. Most adults who watched the coverage in the wake of the Murrah Building bombing in Oklahoma City can still recall the graphic images of the severely injured children being rescued from the rubble. This emotional reaction is more pronounced as the age of the victims decreases. As younger children are even more innocent and incapable of protecting themselves, our reaction to their suffering is even more pronounced.

Terrorist attacks on school children draw intensive media coverage. As we saw with the attack in Beslan, the media coverage of the atrocity was graphic and continual even though it took place during a time when there were numerous significant events that were newsworthy. A danger of this type of media response is that it demonstrates to terrorists that an attack on school children is likely to result in intensive media coverage.

SOFT TARGETS

Taking these factors into account, it becomes apparent that elementary schools and school buses can be particularly attractive targets to terrorists. Crises at elementary schools instantly evoke a stronger emotional response and rapidly draw media coverage. At the same time, elementary schools are typically the softest targets. Very few have a dedicated school resource officer on staff or have established other security measures which are more common at middle and high schools. School buses also present an extremely vulnerable target with high symbolic value. In most parts of this country, we see school buses every school day. An attack on a school bus anywhere would find us being constantly reminded of the attack as we observed buses in our community. As we look at the relatively small number of school related terrorism incidents around the globe, a pattern emerges where elementary schools and buses used to transport children (including commuter buses) appear to have been targeted at a higher rate.

ATTEMPTS TO DRAW SCRUTINY ON GOVERNMENT

Perhaps when terrorists do select school children as targets for their attacks, they are influenced by a perception that the government targeted by the attack will be viewed by supporters as having harmed children themselves. For example, Palestinian terrorists have often maintained that Israeli Defense Forces personnel have killed innocent children in their military actions to combat terrorism. In the minds of terrorists and at least some supporters, this type of contention may make the suffering of innocent children acceptable because the children's suffering is linked to the government they are attacking.

A RATIONALIZATION FOR VIOLENCE

Regardless of the motivation, terrorists who attack children clearly have the ability to justify in their minds that the terrible pain they inflict is an acceptable cost in the furtherance of their objectives. Keeping in mind that many terrorists and their organizations are ruthless in their efforts, schools and school children may seem as natural a target as any. Fortunately, most people around the world maintain the conviction that children should not be pawns in the deadly games played by terrorists.

Chapter 6

Reaction – The Importance of Effective Response

Before looking at ways in which we may respond to acts of terrorism, it is important to look at the experiences of others both nationally and internationally. In order to gain insight and information from those who have experienced acts of terrorism, co-author Michael Dorn spent fourteen days completing intensive training and attending briefings from the Israel Police, Israel Defense Forces and Israeli intelligence services. In addition, as a delegate in the Georgia International Law Enforcement Exchange Program (GILEE), he had the opportunity to visit police and military facilities, and to interact with a wide variety of personnel from these agencies. For American law enforcement executives, the program provides a much better understanding of terrorism though obviously from the Israeli perspective. Both coauthors have had the opportunity to provide training to high-ranking police officials from Israel when they were in the United States through the GILEE program. This program also afforded additional opportunities to learn about terrorism from these experienced professionals. We have found these opportunities to be invaluable. As one ranking Israeli police official told our group, "Israel does not claim to be the best at combating terrorism, but we are among the most experienced." There is definite value in examining the lessons learned in Israel as well as in other countries where terrorism has been more prevalent.

One key lesson learned from this experience was the emphasis placed on the governmental reactions to terrorism

"We cannot afford to wait until the day of an emergency or crisis to develop a response plan or relationships. We need to plan well in advance of an emergency or crisis and develop those relationships which will prove to be critical during a crisis in the community."
Ed Clarke
Director from the Department of School Safety and Security. Montgomery County, MD.

and just as importantly, the reaction of the general populace to incidents of terrorism. During GILEE briefings, senior Israeli police officials maintained that both the economy and the system of government in Israel are more vulnerable to outside influences than that of the United States and many other countries. They describe the economy as more fragile and their system of government as much more diverse and complex with numerous political parties.

Israeli officials came to the conclusion many years ago that the reaction of government officials and of the general public could cause more damage to the state of Israel than the terrorist acts themselves. Though, clearly, it is of utmost importance to consider the human suffering that occurs in a terrorism event and to honor its victims, it is, likewise, important to consider the aims of terrorism. Through shock and fear generated by terrorist acts, terrorists often attempt to destabilize the targeted society and its governmental structure as well as negatively impact its economy. It is essential, therefore, that both the general public and the government act in a way that minimizes the overall impact of terrorism and reduces its damage to political and economic stability.

RETURNING TO BUSINESS AS USUAL

Israeli police officials stressed to our group the need for citizens, businesses, governmental agencies and other impacted groups and organizations to return to normal business and daily routines as quickly as possible after an attack. They maintained that if this is not accomplished, the impact of the actual incident is greatly increased. For example, in one briefing, we were shown crime scene pictures of a terrorist bombing of an outdoor market with considerable damage to the area. A number of victims were killed and injured in the attack. We were then shown photographs of the same market filled with merchants and shoppers. We were told that these photographs were taken later in the same day after the bombing occurred. This reaction to a terrorism event is intended to minimize damage to the Israeli economy and to demonstrate to terrorists that the attack did not have the desired effect. The U.S. government's response after the September 11th 2001 attacks shared some similarities. The public was quickly advised to try to get back to business as usual. This approach is consistent with what we learned from our research on the topic of terrorism. A society that allows acts of terrorism to significantly disrupt how people function on a daily basis may increase the likelihood of future attacks and may cause significantly magnified negative affects from those attacks. Terrorists may become encouraged when they see that an attack is having a dramatic effect on the populace. Such a response increases the likelihood that terrorists will attempt more attacks of the same type. It is also important to note that the disruption caused by an attack could also cause more long-term and overall harm than the attack itself.

DAMAGE DONE BY PERSONS POSING AS 'EXPERTS'

On the other hand, irresponsible statements by unqualified individuals at school safety conferences and in media interviews have caused considerable damage. When those who falsely purport to be terrorism experts are quoted on national television or in papers across the nation, they have frequently furthered the aims of terrorists by creating an unrealistic picture of the actual level of risk. In addition, these individuals do not have access to intelligence information that can more accurately forecast what may or may not happen. For this reason, we will make no attempt in this book or in our presentations to predict possible future school related terrorism events. Rather, it is our goal to increase awareness and to help identify the skills needed to prevent, reduce the impact of and recover from any potential terrorist incident.

THE IMPORTANCE OF SAFE SCHOOL PLANNING

The connection between reactions to terrorism and its overall impact makes not only our reaction to terrorism but our advance preparation to respond to and recover from terrorism events critical. School related incidents of terrorism are no exception to these concerns. The safe school planning measures recommended throughout this book are designed, not only to prevent death and injury, but also to minimize the short and long term damage from an event as well. By using the United States Department of Education and Jane's models for safe school plan development, school and public safety officials work together to create a com-

> "Israel serves as a test ground or field laboratory for terrorists. Techniques used there have been transferred to other countries in the past once they worked in Israel."
> Dr. Robert Friedmann

"The safe school planning measures recommended throughout this book are designed, not only to prevent death and injury, but also to minimize the short and long term damage from an event as well."

prehensive approach to the concerns of terrorism and for other types of crises. The Jane's model is based upon and consistent with the United States Department of Education but is much more detailed. The Department of Education's guide was designed to allow time pressed school and public safety officials to gain a solid understanding of the community-based four-phase all hazards approach in a one to two hour period of time. The length, formatting and content of the guide serve this purpose well. The 450 page Jane's guide uses the Department of Education's approach but provides much more detailed and specific information along with many examples of safety plan components. These models emphasize the need to address terrorism concerns *within the all hazards plan* rather than in addition to it. This is a crucial point in terms of our reaction to terrorism events. When school and public safety officials become too focused on any one type of hazard such as multiple victim shootings or acts of terrorism, their overall approach to safety suffers. A major concern in the reaction to school-related terrorism events is that available resources will be inefficiently utilized because of an alarmist reaction to a perceived threat.

USING RESOURCES EFFECTIVELY

Examples of ineffective use of resources during a major school related terrorism event include the reactions of some following the Columbine school shooting and bombing. One Oklahoma school board in a rural community pressured their school superintendent to have helicopter landing pads constructed at each school. Board members had been so impacted by the graphic media images of the Columbine incident that they wanted to be ready if helicopters ever needed to land on their campuses. Fortunately, the superintendent understood that this would be a significant misallocation of resources. He successfully persuaded his board that there were far more efficient ways to use available funding to enhance safety. He also was able to help them understand that not only were the chances that they would ever be used remote, but that by collaborating with local emergency response officials, he had learned if they ever did need to land helicopters on campus, pilots did not need a cement landing pad.

We have seen similar reactions to concerns of school related terrorism already. We have worked with schools and school districts where serious incidents of other types were already occurring, and/or where serious hazards were not being addressed and significant resources were being devoted to limited focus antiterrorism efforts instead of addressing the clearly present hazards. This is where the all hazards approach based on a formal threat and vulnerability assessment can prove to be invaluable. Schools can best work to prevent and become prepared to respond to and recover from incidents of terrorism by implementation of measures that should already be in place but are lacking. For example, the superintendent of a large urban school system was impressed with a demonstration by a vendor selling a sophisticated software emergency response program. The superintendent was very concerned about the possibility of an act of terrorism in his community. While the product was very well designed from a technology standpoint, impressive to look at to those who have not been properly trained in safe school planning, and would appear to be a quick way to enhance a district's readiness for an event, it had serious design flaws. More importantly, the district did not have a written safe schools plan. To expend available resources on this type of product when school officials have not even formed a multidisciplinary safe school planning team and conducted a hazard and vulnerability assessment would not only be fiscally irresponsible, it would be counterproductive. For a fraction of the cost of the system, school and community emergency response officials could dramatically improve their level of safety and preparedness.

Proper implementation of the United States Department of Education and Jane's models allows a community to maximize the use of available resources, reduce the cost of safety measures, significantly reduce the risk of injury and death for students and staff, develop more effective working relationships between school and emergency response officials and dramatically improve the response to and recovery from any major crisis event.

Here are but a few examples of how this approach is effective in addressing terrorism concerns while also addressing more common and prevalent threats:

> "Schools can best work to prevent and become prepared to respond to and recover from incidents of terrorism by implementation of measures that should already be in place but are lacking."

> "Security measures implemented based on the risks identified during the hazard and vulnerability assessment process will not only make it harder for terrorists to conduct surveillance of a school and more difficult for them to carry out most types of attacks, these measures will also reduce the risks associated with bullying, intruders, weapons on campus, gang activity and other more traditional concerns."

- The security measures implemented based on the risks identified during the hazard and vulnerability assessment process will not only make it harder for terrorists to conduct surveillance of a school and more difficult for them to carry out most types of attacks, these measures will also reduce the risks associated with bullying, intruders, weapons on campus, gang activity and other more traditional concerns.

- The type of media protocol developed by most districts that use this approach would be of great benefit in the event of an accident or natural disaster (such as a tornado strike) at a school as well as an incidence of terrorism. The manner in which school and public safety officials handle the release of information can dramatically impact their handling of any crisis and would be particularly important in the event of an act of terrorism. This type of emergency preparedness is addressed when the emergency operations plan is developed.

- In the event of an earthquake, school officials will need to utilize the incident command system that will be relied upon by local, state and federal emergency response personnel. This system is designed to allow all participating organizations to work together efficiently and under extremely difficult conditions. Incident command has also proven to be extremely important when acts of terrorism occur. The response plan under these models includes implementation and application of incident command.

- In one multiple victim school shooting, a number of individuals who were affected by the event committed suicide over the next few years. Having a written recovery plan and a properly trained crisis response team as outlined in the models can help to effectively address these types of incidents as well as any type of terrorism event.

THE PUBLIC'S ROLE

Like the reaction of government agencies and officials, the reactions of the public to an act of terrorism can be very important. Public response to a terrorism event is heavily influenced by the reaction of government officials not only in the community where the attack occurs, but across the nation as well. The time for school and emergency response officials to address these issues is before, not during an incident.

Chapter 7

School Buses and Terrorism

Since the earliest instances of school related terrorism, school buses have been vulnerable to terrorist attack. When Palestinian terrorists murdered nine children and three adults on May 8, 1970 and crippled nineteen other victims for life, they demonstrated that a school bus could quickly become the scene of horror. Terrorists in Russia, Thailand, the West Bank, Djibouti and Somalia have also found school buses to be desirable and vulnerable targets.

SCHOOL BUS AS A VISIBLE SYMBOL

As an extension of the school itself, school buses in our country are a highly symbolic, plentiful, and lightly protected target for terrorists who intend to commit a high profile attack with relatively few resources. As we have seen in numerous school bus hijackings carried out by students and common criminals, American school buses are no less vulnerable than those in other countries. If a student armed with a sword can take over a school bus and force it to travel from Nevada to California, certainly terrorists – who are better armed, trained and committed to their cause – could do so.

THE SCHOOL BUS TERRORISM THREAT

Fortunately, federal agencies like the Transportation Security Administration (TSA) along with school bus transportation organizations such as the National Association of Pupil Transportation (NAPT) began focusing on the possibility of school bus terrorism as early as 2001. Having presented our

> "As an extension of the school itself, school buses in our country are a highly symbolic, plentiful and lightly protected target for terrorists who intend to commit a high profile attack with relatively few resources."

school buses and terrorism sessions at state pupil transportation associations, the NAPT annual conference and at the *School Transportation News Conference,* the co-authors have found that school transportation and law enforcement officials are deeply concerned about the potential for school bus terrorism in this country. Fortunately, school transportation personnel are among the most focused on safety in the school community. In our training sessions with drivers, supervisors and directors around the nation, we have found them to be among those most hungry for information relating to safety and keenly aware of school buses' vulnerabilities.

While we are not predicting acts of school bus terrorism in the United States, the pattern of incidents around the globe indicates that if terrorists chose to target American school children in the future, it would not be unusual for school bus incidents to be among the types of attacks we could see. And, unlike some of the other countries that have experienced terrorist attacks aimed at children on buses, American pupil transportation is more clearly defined in most areas of the country. In many countries, large numbers of school children ride commercial transit buses to school whereas American children more typically ride dedicated and very easily discernable yellow school buses. The clear definition of the American school bus – its visual and symbolic distinction – as well as its constant presence adds to its value as a target.

A Need For Adequate Training

Though strides have been made in the field of pupil transportation antiterrorism, American school bus drivers, overall, still lack a level of training in antiterrorism considerations comparable to their counterparts in other threatened countries. Our buses are also not equipped with armor as school buses in the territories of Israel are. While research has been conducted on how our buses can be armored and an increasing number of districts provide training for their drivers on techniques such as visual weapons screening to enable their drivers to spot an individual with a concealed firearm at or near a bus stop, the fortunate lack of terrorist attacks on American school buses also means our buses and drivers are easier targets than their foreign counterparts in countries such as Israel. However, as effective antiterrorism includes the wise use of antiterrorism measures, some of the measures that have been adopted in Israel are not practical or appropriate for use in the United States at the present time.

TECHNOLOGY AS A TRANSPORTATION SECURITY AID

An increasing number of school systems are investing in new technology and techniques to target harden their buses from threats and to increase their ability to respond to crises which include the threat of terrorism. For example, new technology and techniques such as security cameras which allow the driver to view blind spots on their bus, electronic tracking systems and rooftop numbering of buses to enable police helicopters to quickly identify a bus affected by crisis from the air are becoming more common. More school systems also emphasize the security of buses after hours and have improved security of bus storage facilities. School transportation personnel around the country have become more aware of the need to remain vigilant for any indications that someone is conducting surveillance of bus routes or making unusual inquiries about the transportation of school children.

"School transportation personnel around the country have become more aware of the need to remain vigilant for any indications that someone is conducting surveillance of bus routes or making unusual inquiries about the transportation of school children."

BACKGROUND INVESTIGATIONS FOR SCHOOL BUS DRIVERS

Transportation directors have also, in many cases, intensified their efforts to conduct thorough background checks on applicants for employment. Aware that the 1970 attack we examined at the beginning of this chapter involved efforts by terrorists to gain access to information relating to the bus schedule, America's transportation directors have become even more keenly aware of the need to carefully screen employees. In 2004 the FBI arrested a former school bus driver who had a hazardous materials driver's license on charges stemming from false statements to members of the FBI joint terrorism task force. This incident sent shockwaves through the pupil transportation industry when it was reported in the September issue of *School Transportation News*. Though the FBI has not released any information to indicate that the suspect, Mohammad Kamel Elzahabi, was involved with any plan to carry out an attack involving a school bus, the reports that he served as an instructor at a terrorist training camp in Afghanistan and had connections to al Qaeda cause transportation officials concern.

INVOLVING PUPIL TRANSPORTATION IN SAFE SCHOOL PLANNING

These issues reveal the critical need for school systems to involve pupil transportation operations in their safe school planning efforts. Pupil transportation should be specifically addressed in the safe schools plan with training for drivers and supervisors, their participation in all appropriate drills and exercises, and the creation of emergency operations plan components specific to the role of drivers during a wide range of emergency situations. For example, while many school districts still do not have any form of emergency plan component for their drivers, more districts are taking an approach similar to that of the Hillsborough County, Florida Public School System and are addressing terrorism concerns in their safe school plans as well as creating custom plan components for transportation personnel. Likely the first district in the nation to complete a four phase plan under the new U.S. Department of Education model, this district received a one million dollar crisis planning grant from the U.S. Department of Education as an aid in their efforts to enhance safety. School Security Services Department Chief David Friedberg, along with his multidisciplinary planning team, has developed an extremely comprehensive safe schools plan which includes ready reference flip charts that are specifically tailored for the district's school bus drivers. As part of his ongoing efforts, Chief Friedberg is also developing specific ready reference flip charts in English and Spanish for custodians, food service employees and other support personnel to go along with the charts that have already been issued to teachers and administrators

Other districts are also properly focusing on buses as a part of their safe school planning effort. One large urban district has equipped all of their school buses with a hidden switch which activates an external emergency light to indicate to police that there is an emergency on the bus. Prudence dictates that we not identify this particular district, but their practice is an excellent one and it demonstrates the district's

> "Pupil transportation should be specifically addressed in the safe schools plan with training for drivers and supervisors, their participation in appropriate drills and exercises, and the creation of emergency operations plan components specific to the role of drivers during a wide range of emergency situations."

commitment to their drivers and the thousands of children they transport each school day.

There are still other instances of effective action. For example, a large district trained and equipped every officer in their school district police force to perform what are known as rapid deployment tactics to aid in neutralizing the threat of an active shooter on a school bus. Officers have been trained and have practiced the techniques not only in area schools but on school buses as well. A relatively new technique for American police personnel that became more common after the Columbine High School attack, rapid deployment tactics have been in use in Israel and other countries prone to terrorism for many years.

PLANNING TO ENHANCE SCHOOL BUS SECURITY

Along with the clear need for schools to incorporate pupil transportation into their comprehensive safe school planning process, there is another important consideration for pupil transportation. School and area public safety officials should meet and discuss ways to dramatically enhance the level of physical security for school buses and school bus stops in the event that an act of terrorism involving a school bus were to occur on American soil. The ability of local school and public safety officials to demonstrate to parents, drivers and students that they have planned for such an eventuality will be needed to reassure them that reasonable efforts are in place to address the suddenly heightened level of concern that such an attack would create. Planning in advance for potential and foreseeable events such as an act of school bus terrorism on American soil will dramatically improve schools' ability to adapt effectively and rapidly to the fears such acts generate.

Combating Terrorism
in Schools

Chapter 8

What Can Schools Do?

No law enforcement officer wants to have to respond to an incident of terrorism at a local school. Similarly, parents shudder to think of such possibilities as they send their children off to school. Our nation's law enforcement officers and other emergency response officials realize that, unfortunately, disaster can strike any school without warning. We have all seen the results of major school crisis situations where innocent children have died and emergency responders have been pushed to their physical and psychological limits. Such disasters may be a tornado, a fire, or a horrific act of violence. A school crisis may strike at any time, be it a Monday morning or a Thursday afternoon. Multiple victim shootings, hostage situations and other terrible events have occurred in private religious schools, rural schools, suburban areas, as well as in urban centers. An earthquake will show no mercy on any school located in its area of devastation. While such tragedies are, thankfully, extremely rare events, they can and do sometimes happen. While remote, no community can afford to ignore these possibilities.

Public safety personnel want to be properly prepared to respond as effectively as possible should tragedy strike a school in their community. They know, deep down, that in the event of a major crisis, there will be no second chance to get it right, little time to stop and think, and that the lives of children will be in their hands. They also know that the outcome of any crisis will be determined largely by advanced

"The events of September 11, have thrust us into a new reality where parents and school officials are worried about their schools being the site of a terrorist attack or event. I suggest that schools need to take an all-hazards approach to deal with all types of incidents."
Gregory Thomas Director, Columbia University's National Center for Disaster Preparedness' School Planning and Preparedness Program

planning efforts, regular drills and exercises as well as training conducted long before that day. Every emergency responder understands that the children of their community are among the most vulnerable citizens that they are hired to protect. School officials have many allies to turn to as they strive to prevent, mitigate, prepare for, respond to and recover from school crisis situations. They understand that the dedicated men and women of America's public safety agencies will respond when our children are in danger.

School safety is the business, not only of school officials, but of law enforcement officers, paramedics, firefighters, emergency management personnel, public health officials, mental health professionals and a host of other local, state and federal experts. Students, parents, and community resource agencies also can and do help make our schools safer when given the chance. Preventing tragedy and helping schools prepare to face major crisis situations is within the domain of every public safety employee and, in effect, every citizen. The general public as well as professionals around the nation will judge those who are charged with the protection of our children by how well a major school crisis situation is handled should it take place in your community. And now the bar by which your communities' ability to protect children, not only from acts of terrorism, but every other hazardous event, has been raised.

In May, 2003, the United States Department of Education released the agency's most comprehensive publication ever relating to the development of a safe schools plan. *Practical Information on Crisis Planning: a Guide for Schools and Communities,* (www.ed.gov/emergencyplan/), was developed over the period of nearly a year by expert working groups comprised of more than thirty top professionals from many disciplines. This guide details a number of critical concepts, among them the need for school officials to involve emergency response officials in their prevention and emergency preparedness efforts. Experts have long contended that only comprehensive and community – based safe schools plans tailored to fit the needs of the individual community are effective. This guide recommends that the all hazards approach to safe school planning be utilized.

> "School officials need to work with the idea of partnering with emergency personnel and other stakeholders in the disaster preparedness process. How to create mutual understanding between and among stakeholders, when to do it, and what the relationships will consist of is required. These concepts are presented often. Yet the actual "nuts and bolts" of getting it done are elusive."
> Nancy Degnan, PhD

Per the guide's recommendation, the plan should address all types of hazards that can occur in the local community rather than focusing on a few types of crises that happen to hold the public's attention due to media exposure of a few high profile events. A proper all hazards plan will address incidents of terrorism just as it addresses natural disasters. While some may advocate that a special terrorism plan be developed, leading experts contend that this is not only a waste of time and resources, but may prove to be counter-productive. With some types of terrorism incidents, it may not be immediately apparent that terrorism is involved at the onset. For example, if a terrorist group set off an explosion and ruptured a chemical storage tank in proximity to a school, the principal would, most likely, not know that they were faced with an act of terrorism. What they would quickly realize, however, is that a dangerous airborne substance posed a threat to their students and staff. Under the all hazards approach to planning, they would be provided with exact protocols guiding their actions in response to the specific threat they faced. This approach is not only more effective during an actual event, but saves considerable time and expenditure of resources in the preparation phase.

Members of the expert working groups expressed significant concerns that school systems around the country have frequently taken the easy, but sometimes deadly, approach of utilizing the 'plan in a can.' A 'plan in a can' is a generic, one size fits all, response plan that is often purchased from a vendor or simply copied from another school district. Many schools rely on such plans without tailoring them to the unique risks and resources of their community. While planning systems and templates can save significant time and money, simply copying or purchasing a plan provides a false sense of security. If local experts were not involved with the development of the safe schools plan for area public and private schools, the plans are not what they could and should be. In such cases, not only the reputation of communities, but the safety of emergency officials and the children they are trying to save will be at risk if disaster strikes.

Unfortunately, most school systems have incomplete safe schools plans. For example, many school systems have a

> "While some may advocate that a special terrorism plan be developed, leading experts contend that this is not only a waste of time and resources, but may prove to be counterproductive."

"A safety and security plan that sits on the shelf has no value." Ada Dolch United States Department of Education adjunct trainer and former Principal for the High School for Leadership and Public Service located a few hundred yards from ground zero.

detailed emergency operations plan but lack a written prevention plan. According to the guide, a proper safe schools plan fully addresses the four phases of emergency management:

Mitigation/prevention

Preparedness

Response

Recovery

Having formally reviewed many safe schools plans from around the nation as well as having responded after the fact to provide support in hundreds of school crisis situations, we would estimate that less than one in one hundred school systems and private schools has a plan that properly addresses these four critical phases.

There was also a strong consensus among the participants in the expert working groups and development team members from the Department of Education that comprehensive all hazards plans were often lacking, representing a critical gap in many communities. The Department of Education guide is the best effort yet by the federal government to outline concepts for the creation of a plan designed for results rather than for show. By including such local experts as law enforcement officers, emergency management officials and mental health experts, the document covers many critical concepts that have been sorely lacking in previous efforts. For example, William Modzeleski, the Associate Under Secretary, Office of Safe and Drug – Free Schools, listened to working group members with law enforcement and emergency management backgrounds and made the concept of incident command an integral part of the emergency preparedness section of the guide. While educators might feel that this is a minor point, any fire service or law enforcement officer knows that an understanding of incident command is a core competency issue for those with command responsibility. A school administrator who tries to manage a major incident without understanding and working through the local incident command system will fail.

Improved information on safe school planning is also coming from the private sector. In the spring of 2004, Jane's

"The Department of Education guide is the best effort yet by the federal government to outline concepts for the creation of a plan designed for results rather than for show."

Information Group released the results of a massive writing project with three new books on school safety. A highly regarded publisher of military and public safety information, Jane's spared no effort in making sure that the series provides solid and specific information to make our nation's schools safer. The series was authored by four of the nation's most highly credentialed and respected school safety experts and a team of more than thirty reviewers from around the nation who are experienced practitioners from a number of disciplines. The thrust of the project was the *Jane's Safe Schools Planning Guide for All Hazards* (www.janes.com), a large textbook sized guide that provides the most detailed information on safe schools plan development yet produced. The book supports the concepts outlined in the Department of Education guide by providing much greater depth and detail while addressing the four phases of emergency management.

Scott Hayes, Director of Public Safety for Jane's, describes the approach used in the development of this series as "an incredible and ambitious effort to expand upon the excellent work of the United States Department of Education to provide school and public safety officials with the most comprehensive approach to the topic to date. Our team has risen to the challenge and we are pleased with and proud of the results."

With the resources available from the United States Department of Education and private sources such as Jane's, school and public safety personnel have never before had so much information at their disposal to help them support local schools. The safe school plan encompassing all four phases of emergency management is the new paradigm. Communities that have not yet addressed these four critical phases with properly developed safe schools plans will soon find themselves behind the curve. They may also experience the needless loss of children's lives. As the front line of defense for our nation's schools, children and those who dedicate their lives to educating them, our nation's school and emergency response officials cannot afford to lag behind. With the threat of events ranging from natural disasters to acts of terrorism in our schools, now is the time to ensure that reasonable steps are taken to safeguard the schools in your community – the child you save may be your own.

Safe school plan development

Planning teams

"The most
effective way
to develop a
comprehensive
plan as described
by the U.S.
Department of
Education and
Jane's models
is to form a
planning team."

The most effective way to develop a comprehensive plan as described by the U.S. Department of Education and Jane's models is to form a planning team. The team should be chaired by one person who has the appropriate time, authority and resources to dedicate to the project. Seven sub-chairs should then be selected, four to oversee the development of each plan section and three to chair what will become ongoing activities to see that the plan is effectively implemented on an ongoing basis. These chairs and functions include:

Prevention and mitigation plan chair
Preparedness plan chair
Response plan chair
Recovery plan chair
Tactical site survey chair
Crisis response team chair
Exercise program chair

A variety of school and emergency response officials should be selected to serve on the seven committees as needed. There will often be overlap of roles, particularly in smaller communities. For example, the same fire department official may serve on several committees. For this reason, care must be taken to keep the number of meetings to a minimum and to utilize smaller meetings of a few key committee members when appropriate. A low cost planning system such as the one developed by the authors and Sonayia Shepherd can provide a starting framework for the project and dramatically reduce planning time while allowing for the creation of a customized plan. Another approach is to utilize one or more government planning guides and an existing plan as a starting point. If this approach is utilized, great care must be taken to avoid the tendency for people not to think beyond the example they are starting with. Committee chairs should emphasize that these documents are simply a place to start in the process. Properly developed planning templates and guides tend to be more effective as they provide a range of options in terms of plan component format to choose from. This process tends to force planning teams to create a customized plan rather than to simply copy.

THE PREVENTION AND MITIGATION PLAN

One of the easiest plan sections to develop, the prevention and mitigation plan is simply a compilation of measures that are in place in area schools to prevent and mitigate against accidents, fire, the effects of natural disasters and acts of violence including terrorism. The process of creating this plan does not require as much creative effort as the team is listing current practices rather than creating a series of action steps and protocols as in the preparedness phase. This process helps to identify weaknesses in the prevention and mitigation strategy, provides clearer written guidance for school officials, creates a document that can be used by school system legal counsel to defend the district in litigation and helps to identify duplication of effort and waste of available resources. It is critical that the prevention and mitigation measures that are described in the document actually reflect current practices.

As with the other plan sections, the prevention and mitigation plan should be reviewed and updated at least once annually. Taking such steps also helps to force school and emergency response personnel to reevaluate safety measures periodically to identify improvements that need to be made.

During this process, all areas of prevention and mitigation should be evaluated. Many of the measures that have proven to be effective for the prevention of more common crimes and acts of violence are also effective at helping to prevent acts of terrorism. While terrorists are often more motivated than the average criminal, they, too, often, seek easy targets. Efforts to regulate access to schools, security cameras, on site police personnel and other target hardening approaches may lead terrorists to select another site that offers fewer obstacles, or in some cases, might lead to the capture of terrorists before they can strike. For example, some terrorist groups have a tendency to conduct surveillance of potential targets. The use of standard prevention measures, such as careful screening of applicants for employment and contractors or proper access control, may lead to the arrest of ter-

> "As with the other plan sections, the prevention and mitigation plan should be reviewed and updated at least once annually. Taking such steps also helps to force school and emergency personnel to reevaluate safety measures periodically to identify improvements that need to be made."

rorists who are trying to gain access to a school to conduct surveillance. While it can be extremely difficult to prevent an act of terrorism at the level of the targeted site, there have been instances where prevention and mitigation efforts have been effective in preventing or minimizing the effects of an attempted attack.

PREPAREDNESS PLAN

The preparedness phase is typically the most difficult in terms of plan development. The reason for this difficulty? An entire series of procedures in the form of protocols must be developed. The need to make sure that all components of the plan are in agreement with one another also makes the development of this plan time and labor intensive. For example, a proper plan will consist of a system-wide plan supported by a series of supplemental plan components such as flip charts. The flip charts must be developed from and match the action steps in the system plan or inconsistency in response efforts will result. Flip charts should be developed for various categories of employees such as administrators, teachers, custodians and school bus drivers since each has different roles during a crisis. A good quality set of templates can be quite helpful – as matching templates can be used to easily create the system plan and the appropriate flip charts.

The heart of the preparedness effort is the emergency operations plan, sometimes referred to as a crisis plan. This plan consists of a series of integrated components including:

- **The system plan**: This standardized set of protocols guides the actions of employees for all schools and facilities in the district.

- **Site procedures**: Typically a one page supplement inserted after each protocol to tailor the plan to each unique school or facility. The site procedures are developed at the building level when the completed system plan is issued to each site. Site procedures for each building should include a printed photo tour of the facility. Using a digital camera, a photo album is created that will allow emergency responders to quickly become familiar with the facility. Creation of this visual tool can be critically important for certain situations such as a disaster where there is extensive damage to the facility. While electronic format tours are also valuable, a printed version should always be on hand.

- **Ready reference flip charts**: Are a condensed version of the system plan created for primary categories of employees such as teachers, administrators and bus drivers. Each version of the flip chart spells out the appropriate action steps for that category of employee. Flip charts describing employee specific action steps are a critical part of the plan as bus drivers and teachers carry out different functions during the same crisis. Note: with rare exceptions such as extremely small private schools, a flip chart is **not adequate as a plan in and of itself** but should be viewed as a supplement to the primary plan. While extremely valuable as a tool, flip charts cannot contain enough information to serve as a complete plan.

- **Electronic virtual tours**: Virtual tours of each facility and type of school bus can be created to enhance the plan dramatically. These can be stored on CD-ROM, keychain jump drives and on websites with secure access. As with the printed version, these should include photos of all critical equipment with instructions for emergency operations. For example, providing a photo of the fire sprinkler control system with instructions for turning the system on and off.

Formatting of the plan is crucial if a plan is going to be easy to use under stress. The best format relies on the use of two types of protocols, functional protocols and incident specific protocols. Functional protocols are specific procedures that outline in step-by-step fashion those action steps that should be performed to carry out specific emergency functions such as a lockdown or emergency evacuation. The functional protocols should be placed in the front of the plan and training efforts and drills should be focused heavily on the functional protocols. If teachers and other staff can readily carry out the functional protocols, they are well on their way to being prepared for any type of crisis. Incident specific protocols are those procedures that are designed for specific types

> "Formatting of the plan is crucial if a plan is going to be easy to use under stress."

of incidents such as a hazardous materials incident, tornado or fire. The incident specific protocols list implementation of the functional protocols and other more specific steps as their action steps.

The emergency operations plan components should cover special needs persons, after hours and special events, school bus incidents and incidents that occur off campus but that will affect the school. The plan should be designed so that it is extremely easy to use by those who are under extreme stress. All school employees should receive training on the plan and plans should be tested through a series of progressively more difficult exercises as described later in this chapter.

RESPONSE PLAN

"While there are a variety of available options, the response plan is basically a plan to ensure that the emergency operations plan is properly executed and that key actions are properly documented."

While there are a variety of available options, the response plan is basically a plan to ensure that the emergency operations plan is properly executed and that key actions are properly documented. This plan is easier to develop because it is based upon and created from the emergency operations plan. The response plan can be a simple series of checklists with places to record which actions were taken by what people or agencies and what time they were taken. This plan creates redundancy which is needed to ensure that critical action steps are carried out under stressful and sometimes chaotic conditions. Planners should keep in mind that under actual crisis conditions, school staff members may lose much of their cognitive reasoning ability.

RECOVERY PLAN

As with prevention and mitigation plans, it is unfortunate that the majority of public school systems and private schools in this country do not have a written recovery plan. The recovery plan is necessary because students, staff and their loved ones are often heavily traumatized by major crisis events. A written recovery plan helps to ensure that proper recovery measures and techniques are effectively utilized after a traumatic event. During the recovery planning process, appropriate measures as well as the personnel who will carry them out are identified and recorded.

Suicides and other negative results have occurred following major school crisis situations. The emotional damage resulting from a major school crisis can be extensive and careful pre-incident planning is needed to help address it. As with other planning steps, school officials should take great care to identify the right people to help in recovery plan development. Just as a mental health professional or educator may not be qualified to develop certain emergency procedures, people who are trained and experienced in crisis response and recovery should be involved in the development of the recovery plan.

The four sections of the plan, as a whole, constitute the safe schools plan. Care should be taken to properly separate out the information that needs to be in each plan. For example, prevention and mitigation measures should not be included in the emergency operations plan as they will only make it more difficult to use under stress.

The remaining three teams are developed and maintained to ensure that the plan is properly implemented and that safety is continually evaluated:

TACTICAL SITE SURVEY TEAM

A tactical site survey is an annual multidisciplinary crisis preplanning session conducted in concert with a hazard and vulnerability assessment of each school and facility owned/ or leased by the district. This process is used to record critical information that will be needed by school and emergency response officials during the response phase. The survey is also designed to identify any hazardous conditions that exist and to find ways to correct them. Safety measures such as the purchase of security equipment should be based on the results of tactical site surveys. The team should also evaluate the most recent community hazard assessment. This assessment is typically coordinated by the local emergency management agency. The community hazard assessment and tactical site survey results should drive the planning process and guide decisions relating to safety training of school staff, safety policy and purchase of safety equipment. The tactical site survey is one of the most critical and effective safety strategies available. A free tactical site survey checklist can be downloaded at www.schoolterrorism.com (click on the Free Resources tab).

CRISIS RESPONSE TEAM

The crisis response team consists of a district wide team and a team at each school and facility. Team members are responsible for implementing the emergency operations plan, response plan and the recovery plan. The district team is comprised of district wide personnel and members from the building teams. The district team helps to support the building team of affected schools should they experience a crisis. Crisis response team members should receive appropriate training and be afforded the opportunity to practice their skills through participation in the exercise program.

EXERCISE PROGRAM

Over the years, the emergency management community has developed specific types of exercises that are designed to be used in a progressive exercise program over time to help test plans and to allow staff to practice implementing them. Unfortunately, exercises are often conducted improperly with less than desirable results.

Untested emergency operations plans are only effective 'in theory' and most often fail during school crisis events. Testing of such plans occurs through the conduct of mock crisis exercises. Schools across the country have conducted these kinds of exercises to increase their readiness for crisis situations. However, there are potential pitfalls that can occur when exercises are not conducted properly.

In all probability, the most common and significant problem with school crisis exercises, occurs when they are conducted before the school emergency operations plan has been completed and prior to personnel being trained on their roles in an emergency. This practice can result in the testing of untrained people rather than the testing of the emergency operations plan. Instead, a series of properly designed and carefully developed exercises should be used. When methods that have been developed by the emergency management community are used, safe and effective exercises are possible.

Local, state, and federal emergency management agencies can provide valuable expertise in selecting, developing, and

> Does every individual in your school, who will have to respond at the time of a crisis or emergency, know the plan? How often is the plan reviewed with staff, students, custodians and kitchen personnel?
> Ada Dolch
> United States Department of Education adjunct trainer and former Principal for the High School for Leadership and Public Service located a few hundred yards from ground zero.

coordinating exercises. While available assistance will vary from one region to another, a little research can determine where assistance can be found. Qualified consultants with an emergency management background can also be helpful. Local organizations such as airports and hospitals are often required to complete exercises periodically and schools may benefit by partnering with the local emergency management agency to observe and even participate in these exercises.

There are several exercise types that have specific advantages and best serve certain functions. The following is a greatly abbreviated description of the standard exercise types and their functions from the Federal Emergency Management Agency *Exercise Design Course* Student Manual:

> **Orientation seminar** – This is a low stress, informal discussion in a group setting used to help participants from all involved agencies understand roles, plans, and equipment that would come into play during a crisis. An orientation seminar serves as an opportunity to resolve coordination issues and to make sure that responsibilities are assigned. This type of meeting is useful to review new procedures, plans, or policies, and helps to prepare for more complex exercises.

> **Drill** – Schools routinely conduct fire and severe weather drills. A drill is simply a coordinated and supervised activity to check out a specific operation or function in one agency such as a school or a police department. Drills are useful to allow personnel to get familiar with new equipment, procedures, or to practice and maintain current skills. Drills are an excellent way to test specific new concepts in an emergency operations plan to see how they would work.

> **Tabletop exercise** – These exercises should be used much more frequently in the school setting than they often are. Tabletop exercises provide an opportunity for all relevant agencies to test their ability to implement emergency operation plans with low stress, low cost, and less chance of being embarrassed publicly by trying to execute a poorly planned full scale exercise. This kind of exercise involves the simulation of a crisis situation

Prepare, communicate, practice, practice
Ada Dolch
United States Department of Education adjunct trainer and former Principal for the High School for Leadership and Public Service located a few hundred yards from ground zero.

On 9-11 when there was no use of a telephone for communications purposes, we were able to stay in touch because the radios we had purchased became our line of communication. The frequent drills allowed everyone to know what to do as a routine and not as a surprise.
Ada Dolch
United States Department of Education adjunct trainer and former Principal for the High School for Leadership and Public Service located a few hundred yards from ground zero.

in an informal and stress-free setting. The participants talk through issues and work together toward solutions of problems that are posed by the scenario. It is a low-key means to identify areas that need improvement and helps to build working relationships between agencies that will respond during a crisis.

Functional exercise – This is often the most productive type of exercise for schools and is unfortunately the least commonly utilized. A functional exercise is a fully simulated interactive exercise that occurs in real time sequence with a high degree of stress and realism. These exercises are the most realistic type of multi-agency exercise short of the full scale exercise. Functional exercises are normally conducted in an emergency operations center setting using messages that are delivered to role players by other personnel acting in the capacity of simulators. A well designed functional exercise will identify oversights so they can be corrected prior to conducting a full-scale exercise.

Full-scale exercise – A properly designed full-scale exercise is the closest simulation of a real disaster possible. It will often take 6 to 12 months of preparation using combinations of the types of exercises described previously to prepare to conduct a well run full-scale exercise. A full-scale exercise is a relatively time consuming and expensive activity due to the number of resources that must be committed. These exercises are normally implemented after other basic issues have been thoroughly addressed. Although it is tempting to prematurely jump to this phase of disaster preparation, it can be counterproductive and even dangerous to do so. There are many safety and public relations considerations when a full scale exercise is used. A police officer was shot and killed during an improperly conducted full scale exercise at a Texas school and several instances of civil litigation have occurred when full scale exercises were conducted without following standard practices such as marking all participants and carefully controlling access to the exercise site. Full scale exercises should and can be used, but they are a final step in a gradual series of exercises.

School emergency exercises can be an excellent means to test emergency operations plans and to provide valuable practice to potential responders. No school is ready for a major crisis until appropriate exercises have been conducted. If the concepts that have been painstakingly developed by the emergency management discipline are followed, exercises can be extremely beneficial for any school.

By using the all hazards model to safe school planning, the level of risk, ability to properly respond to and means of recovering from any school crisis situation including an act of terrorism will be dramatically improved. As we have emphasized, local emergency response officials must be involved in this planning effort. The time for school and public safety officials to discuss what to do to prevent, prepare for, respond to and recover from an act of terrorism is before, not during an incident.

According to the new paradigm, no safe schools plan is complete unless it includes written and detailed information to address all four phases of emergency management:

- **Prevention/Mitigation** – a written strategy to prevent injuries, deaths and loss of or damage to property and to reduce the negative impact of natural disasters and other harmful events.

- **Preparedness** – The development of a written emergency operations plan and supporting emergency preparedness measures to see that it can be effectively implemented under actual crisis conditions.

- **Response** – Guidance for all school staff on how the written procedures in the emergency operations plan can be successfully implemented in the event of an emergency, crisis or disaster.

- **Recovery** – Detailed and written advance preparations to guide school, mental health and other officials through the process to help schools impacted by a crisis recover from crisis situations.

Sources: Michael Dorn, Gregory Thomas, Marleen Wong and Sonayia Shepherd – *Jane's Safe Schools Planning Guide for All Hazards (2004)* and *Practical Information on Crisis Planning: a Guide for Schools and Communities* United States Department of Education (2003).

The four phases referenced in the above text box are a continual process. It is imperative that school officials, employees, emergency responders and related agencies within the community work continually to develop, refine and improve this integral plan.

TERRORISM CONCERNS – DEFINITIONS AND RESOURCES

There are vast resources available to aid campus safety professionals in addressing terrorism concerns. Free manuals, government funded training, privately available training and consulting services, books, web sites and a host of other information rich resources are available. School and public safety professionals must exercise care in evaluating the quality, accuracy and applicability of the resource to their situation. By focusing on the needs of the organization as well as the local situation, local officials can more efficiently develop practical and effective measures to reduce risk and to be prepared to respond to and recover from incidents of terrorism. The definitions, concepts and resources provided below may prove to be helpful aids for those tasked with addressing concerns of terrorism on or near schools.

Great care should be taken to match experts to the needs being addressed. For example a counterterrorism expert may be the ideal person to assist school resource officers, school district police officers and university police personnel in developing rapid deployment capabilities to respond to an active shooter situation. But this same expert may not possess the skills required for the development of emergency operations protocols relating to terrorism. Similarly, an antiterrorism expert might prove to be extremely beneficial in emergency preparedness and risk reduction strategies but would likely be limited in their ability to help in the creation of a school system police tactical team. By staying focused on the relevance of expertise, the best fit between the knowledge base required and the concern to be addressed can be made. While some individuals have multiple skill areas, it is important not to fall into the dangerous trap of assuming that a given area of expertise will serve as a viable source for all areas of concern. It is, therefore, a good idea to develop a list of experts and specifically note their areas of expertise as it relates to various aspects of the school safety plan. In this way, you can put your available expertise to its best use while, at the same time, avoid embarrassing information gaps, or worse, a plan based in misinformation.

The following are services that can often be obtained from private consultants and non profit organizations:

Training

Quality training in emergency preparedness, target hardening, tactical response for law enforcement, crisis intervention, weapons screening and a variety of other topical areas can prove to be quite beneficial.

Tactical site surveys

Far more in depth than a 'safety audit,' 'hazard hunt,' or 'site assessment,' a tactical site survey is a thorough risk reduction and emergency preparedness evaluation involving local public safety, emergency management and campus personnel. The tactical site survey is typically the most cost-effective safety measure and should be conducted before security systems and other major purchases are made. A number of consultants provide tactical site survey services and at least one non-profit organization offers a training program to help campus officials internalize the process so they are not dependent on hiring a consulting firm year after year.

Facility plan design reviews

Review of building and site plans by an experienced team, typically an architect working with emergency management and/or antiterrorism specialists, can be one of the wisest expenditures made when designing or renovating a campus facility. Properly conducted plan reviews can save thousands and even millions of dollars, particularly when civil liability issues are considered. When architects are properly trained in this specialty area, a few simple suggestions can avert safety-related building flaws also making the facility a less appealing target for terrorists.

Emergency operations plan reviews

A thorough review of emergency operations plans by a qualified expert or team can quickly identify weaknesses so they can be addressed before an incident occurs. Reviews of this kind can be another extremely cost effective measure.

Crisis intervention training

Proper preparation of crisis team members on techniques that will be needed to address a major incident, particularly if mass casualties result. By conducting a thorough risk assessment and identifying the appropriate resources, campus safety officials can address terrorism concerns in a more effective, rational and time efficient manner.

> "By conducting a thorough risk assessment and identifying the appropriate resources, campus safety officials can address terrorism concerns in a more effective, rational and time efficient manner."

TERRORISM TALK
DEFINITIONS OF BASIC TERRORISM TERMS

Terrorism
According to the Federal Bureau of Investigation, terrorism is "The unlawful use of force against persons or property to intimidate a government, the civilian population or any segment thereof in furtherance of political or social objectives."

Source: Threat and Risk Assessment for Weapons of Mass Destruction course manual – Office of Domestic Preparedness.

Antiterrorism
Efforts to prevent or reduce the impact of terrorism – typically prior to an event

Counterterrorism
Though sometimes used by agencies and individuals to include both antiterrorism and counterterrorism activities, the term has traditionally been used to describe activities including intelligence gathering, investigative efforts and tactical responses by military or law enforcement personnel. Most tactical responses often involve using special equipment and tactics.

Domestic terrorism
Terrorism by terrorist groups within their own country.

International terrorism
Terrorism carried out by terrorists, resources or operational plans that originate from other countries.

Chapter 9

Wolves in Sheep's Clothing

Having worked full time in the field of campus safety for more than twenty-five years, coauthor Michael Dorn has been in the business long enough to interact with most of the nation's top campus safety experts. He has also been in the field long enough to run into a number of charlatans who claim to be school safety experts without adequate basis. Unfortunately, these unscrupulous individuals are not only separating school systems and private schools from their precious limited funds, but they have done considerable damage to the schools they have been hired to help. We are now seeing an extension of this existing problem as these and more individuals of the same ilk exploit the fears of school related terrorism in the same manner.

After the intensive publicity following the string of multiple victim school shootings in the late 1990's, the number of school safety consultants in the United States skyrocketed. As the demand for school safety expertise expanded with the increased fear over school violence events that, in most cases, were not unlike those that had been occurring in this country for several decades, a number of individuals suddenly held themselves out to be school safety experts overnight. As the only requirement for being a school safety consultant is the availability of paying clients, numerous unscrupulous individuals have been cashing in on the opportunity created by the heightened sense of fear among parents and educators. This trend has intensified since the events of September

"As the only requirement for being a school safety consultant is the availability of paying clients, numerous unscrupulous individuals have been cashing in on the opportunity created by the heightened sense of fear among parents and educators."

11, 2001 increased the level of fear of terrorism among school officials, parents and students.

There have been and are a number of school safety consultants who have falsified their credentials. Others, who are experts on one aspect of school safety, regularly work outside of their field of expertise. Likewise, there have been quite a few who routinely plagiarize the work of others who have expertise in the field. Blatant copying of presentations, and other tools developed by experts is sadly common. The major concern with this type of activity is that the individuals rarely fully understand the materials they are plagiarizing and disseminate the information incorrectly.

A few school safety and terrorism "experts" have been working hard to drum up business by predicting a wave of terrorism in our schools. In a United States Secret Service/ United States Department of Education threat management symposium, a participant asked a speaker about the concerns expressed in the media by one "expert" that a certain particularly extreme scenario would be carried out by terrorists. The Secret service agent stated that while such an occurrence was possible, it was highly unlikely. She also stressed that such predictions were not supported by any available reliable intelligence information or past instances of terrorism. She suggested that some consultants might be making statements in media interviews in an attempt to stir up work by instilling unreasonable fears. We could not agree more.

Helping the Terrorists
Sadly, that is part of how terrorism works. Media reports, in some cases, exaggerate the actual individual level of danger from terrorists. An effective act of terrorism creates a level of fear among the affected population that is far greater than the actual level of danger to the average person. This kind of hysteria is, of course, also one of the desired goals in those rare instances where school children are targeted by terrorists.

Ask Questions and Listen Carefully to the Answers
Sonayia Shepherd is a respected colleague who is one of the few people in the country who has actual full time experience working in government units that deal with both school safety and with terrorism. She served as a School Safety

Coordinator for three years and was promoted to the post of State Antiterrorism Planner for the Georgia Emergency Management Agency. She later served as the Bioterrrorism Exercise Coordinator for the Georgia Department of Human Resources. Mrs. Shepherd suggests that before putting stock in the advice of anyone claiming to be a terrorism expert, school officials should ask some basic questions. Does this individual have formal training in antiterrorism or counter-terrorism? If so, who provided the training that makes this individual an authority? Has the expert worked in a full-time capacity in the field of terrorism, and if so, in what capacity? Is their background relevant to the information being provided? By traditional definition, antiterrorism involves efforts to counter, reduce and plan for acts of terrorism while counterterrorism focuses on military or law enforcement tactical responses to acts of terrorism. For example, a retired military officer with experience in counterterrorism operations may be well qualified to advise law enforcement tactical teams, but poorly prepared to help you in school emergency operations planning. A government antiterrorism planner may be extremely helpful in reviewing your school emergency operations plans but might not be qualified to train school resource officers in tactical responses to terrorism incidents. Very few people have solid backgrounds in both antiterrorism and counterterrorism. Even fewer have solid backgrounds in the fields of school safety and antiterrorism or counterterrorism.

> "Media reports, in some cases, exaggerate the actual individual level of danger from terrorists."

VERIFY CREDENTIALS

Before hiring a school safety consultant or contracting with a firm, evaluate their credentials. Be wary of consultants who list vague credentials that would be hard to verify. For example, one consultant refers to himself on his website and in intro-ductions as "Dr." when he, in fact, does not have a doctoral degree. A careful review of his listed credentials reveals that he does not identify a field of study or a specific institution for his graduate degree. The same concept holds true when con-sultants purport to have work experience they do not actually possess. While someone who is actively working as a practi-tioner may not be allowed to mention their specific job title or employing organization in their private work, school officials should be suspicious when the see an individual who lists a credential like "served as a police captain with a metropolitan police force". Most consultants who actually possess the claimed experience will list the agency they worked for or be able to freely provide it when asked. There have been many instances where both private consultants and, in some cases, even government school safety personnel have falsified their credentials in this manner. These types of individuals have even sometimes served as keynote speakers for major professional conferences where conference organizers failed to make reasonable efforts to check out the qualifications of speakers.

> "Another place where we sometimes see people who lack proper qualifications billed as experts is in the media."

Another place where we sometimes see people who lack proper qualifications billed as experts is in the media. There are a variety of professional marketing services designed to help the media identify experts in various fields. Media personnel frequently rely on these services to quickly locate experts to interview for breaking events. While many legitimate experts are listed in these services, there are also those who falsely list themselves as experts. Consultants who are trying to get more work are sometimes motivated to try to generate interviews in this manner. Most of these listing services do not attempt to verify that the customers that pay to be listed actually have the credentials they claim they have and media personnel working on tight deadlines do not always verify that their expert is qualified to serve as a source.

A number of individuals who have falsely claimed to be experts in school safety and terrorism have been featured in interviews on major networks and in print publications. Most importantly, some of these interviews have put out very bad information on the topic of terrorism and schools. When you see an expert interviewed by the media, ask yourself if they are really qualified to address the issue they have been asked to discuss. Often, a careful evaluation of what they say will help to reveal whether they really know what they are talking about or not.

ASK FOR REFERENCES

When hiring a consultant, ask for references who can comment on their services for similar types of work. This will help to eliminate those consultants who are working out of their field of expertise. In one case, a large school system paid a consulting firm more than a million dollars to develop their emergency operations plans. The consulting firm had experience in security consulting but had never worked with a school client before. The plans they developed failed the state review process and have since failed in two actual crisis situations. Had the district asked for previous school client references, they could have avoided this regrettable situation. To make matters worse, this district is now involved in litigation following one of the safety incidents.

USE CONSULTANTS TO INTERNALIZE LONG-TERM CAPACITY

Many consulting firms try to establish client relationships where the school system that retains them must continually pay for their services. For example, they will suggest that the district hire them each year to conduct site surveys. Whenever possible, consultants should be used to help build internal capacity where school and local public safety officials learn to perform the required functions on their own over time. An example of this would be when a school system retains a consulting firm to train local personnel to perform tactical site surveys. For a large district, a team can be trained for a fraction of the cost of site surveys for all of their buildings. This training will enable local personnel to conduct the tactical site surveys at a greatly reduced cost while ensuring that they can be coordinated in future years. When consultants are hired to do the actual work, the district may not be able to maintain the service in coming years due to budget cuts. A quality school safety consulting firm has no shortage of work and will not push clients for services they do not need.

WHAT ARE THE MAIN CONCERNS?

While future events may dictate changes in areas requiring additional attention, there are certain specific points where school officials may want to focus their efforts. These are not limited to the prevention of and preparedness for terrorist events. In fact, as we have seen, good security and emergency preparedness measures designed to reduce risk of terrorism often have much in common with those efforts designed to reduce the risks associated with accidents, typical acts of vio-

> "Evaluating access control, security hardware and the effectiveness of your school/law enforcement partnership can go a long way to target harden your schools."

lence, mass contamination incidents, natural disasters and other hazards of concern. Evaluating access control, security hardware and the effectiveness of your school/law enforcement partnership can go a long way to target harden your schools. Reviewing your emergency operations plans to see how solid protocols are in addressing such key points as bomb threats, major acts of violence, lockdown, evacuation and shelter in place procedures is also a major step in the right direction. In short, there is no need to develop a new emergency operations plan for terrorism. The focus should be on making sure that your existing plan is a good one or on developing a proper all hazards plan. Unfortunately, a number of consultants have been pushing schools to retain them to develop plans that are specific to terrorism. This is not in keeping with best practices such as the U.S. Department of Education planning model.

FOCUS ON THE BASICS FIRST

Dr. Robert Friedmann of Georgia State University serves as the Director of the Georgia International Law Enforcement Exchange Program (GILEE). Through GILEE, hundreds of high ranking police officials from the United States, Israel, Austria and Hungary have traveled to participating countries for intensive training focused on antiterrorism, counterterrorism and community policing. As a trainer for officers coming to the United States and having spent fourteen days in Israel through the program, co-author Michael Dorn can easily state that it is the most intensive of the nearly nineteen months of formal public safety training he received during his two decades in law enforcement. Dr. Friedmann stresses that effective efforts to reduce and respond to terrorism are directly tied to the kinds of measures that we should have in place to address more traditional concerns. Dr. Friedmann emphasizes that community-based efforts like community policing are among our most effective tools to address concerns of terrorism.

While schools have been targeted by terrorists on rare occasions in the past and will likely continue to be in the future, our response must be deliberate and practical. Beware the wolf in sheep's clothing that may be more interested in profits than in the safety of staff and students.

Impacts and Analysis

Chapter 10

Possibilities and Probabilities - What Could Happen?

This chapter is not intended to provide predictions of future school related terrorism events. Instead, it is designed to cover some of the more plausible *possibilities* based on past events and those that could occur due to the amount of information and resources that are or could be available to terrorists. This chapter also includes information on unlikely types of attacks, some of which would be catastrophic in nature. This is important for the emergency preparedness planning effort to be complete. We emphasize that school officials should work closely with area emergency management, law enforcement, fire service, emergency medical services, public health, mental health and other local experts when developing their four phase plan to address these and other potential hazards. We also urge that these plans encompass the possibilities covered in this chapter with an emphasis on those events that are deemed to be *probabilities* based on the multidisciplinary threat and vulnerability process described in the *What Can Schools Do?* chapter.

We would also feel remiss if we did not restate the importance of addressing these issues within the context of a comprehensive all hazards plan in accordance with the United States Department of Education and Jane's models for safe school planning rather than through a separate terrorism plan. As this chapter will illustrate, a number of potential terrorism scenarios would not be immediately apparent as an act of terrorism. As a result of this potential for ambiguity, a school administrator faced with a crisis might not know to

"If using a comprehensive all hazards approach, the administrator would instantly know where to go for the information based on the type of incident they face, such as a hazardous materials release."

consult the terrorism plan. However, if using a comprehensive all hazards approach, the administrator would instantly know where to go for the information based on the type of incident they face, such as a hazardous materials release.

BOMB THREATS AND/OR THE USE OF EXPLOSIVES DEVICES

Historically, explosive devices have been one of terrorists' most favored weapons. Used by terrorists to kill students in two of the attacks on school children by Chechen terrorists as well as by a number of terrorists in Israel, the explosive device is likely to remain a tool of terrorists. Terrorists have used small devices, relatively large devices such as the vehicle bomb detonated in the attack on the Murrah building, the boat bomb used in the attack on the U.S.S. Cole and first World Trade Center attack, as well as man-portable devices strapped to a terrorist. A scenario we have not yet seen but one that could reasonably occur would be for a much larger vehicle bomb such as a tanker truck, being detonated at or near a target on U.S. soil.

"School bomb threat procedures should be designed to make it more difficult for a potential bomber to predict exactly how school officials will respond to each call and more importantly, where students will be located after a call is placed."

Schools should develop thoughtful bomb threat protocols for schools, school owned facilities, school buses and special events. The commonly seen procedure where students are evacuated three hundred feet into a parking lot or athletic field for every bomb threat received would make it extremely easy for a terrorist to inflict casualties by getting school officials to bring victims to the bomb rather than having to try to gain access to plant a device inside the school. As at least one Georgia middle school student has planned such an attack, it would not be unreasonable to envision a trained terrorist using a similar tactic.

School bomb threat procedures should be designed to make it more difficult for a potential bomber to predict exactly how school officials will respond to each call and more importantly, where students will be located after a call is placed. School officials should discuss their options with local, state and federal public safety officials when drafting or revising their bomb threat protocols. Agents from the Bureau of Alcohol, Tobacco and Firearms can provide free training and technical assistance to schools as can many local and state bomb units.

As to prevention measures, these same officials can be valuable resources to school officials. There are a variety of prevention measures that make it harder for a bomber to target a facility. Effective access control, reducing the number of potential hiding places in and around the school, parking control and physical barriers that make it impossible to drive a vehicle into a building are a few examples.

From the standpoint of mitigation, the Federal Emergency Management Agency has developed a guide for designing terrorism resistant schools which includes information on how to design schools that are resistant to damage from explosion.

Though attacks with explosives are difficult to prevent, the chances of a successful attack against a school can be reduced and an effective response to an attack made more likely with proper multidisciplinary planning.

MULTIPLE VICTIM SHOOTING

As we have seen in a number of the incidents around the globe, a sudden firearms attack has also been a favored type of attack with terrorists. American schools often have measures in place to help counter the threat of an active shooter due to the incidents of targeted school violence as defined by the United States Secret Service and the United States Department of Education. One of the more effective countermeasures for this type of assault is keeping an armed school resource officer on campus. At least one mid sized school system equips school police vehicles with rifles, tactical body armor rated to stop rifle fire and ballistic helmets to enhance the ability of officers to neutralize this type of threat. The department has also conducted advanced firearms training to enable officers to utilize the equipment properly if it is ever needed.

Carefully developed lockdown procedures can be an effective mitigation measure as long as staff members have been properly trained and have had an opportunity to practice the procedures with appropriate drills. Again, many American schools have such measures in place due to the concerns of a shooting incident. Another area of concern relating to this type of attack is the vulnerability of students and staff when they are evacuated from a school. There have been at

"Carefully developed lockdown procedures can be an effective mitigation measure as long as staff members have been properly trained and have had an opportunity to practice the procedures with appropriate drills."

least four school shootings carried out by students in the United States where the shooter or shooters first activated the school fire alarm and shot evacuees when they were outside of the building. In November 2003, school resource officers from the Clayton County, Georgia Police Department arrested a student who had planned to lock a series of fire exit doors, activate the fire alarm and shoot students as they were crammed into a central hallway while trying to evacuate. If students have been able to develop this type of plan on multiple occasions around the nation, it is clear that terrorists could as well. School system emergency evacuation protocols should take these and other hazards into account. Evacuees are extremely vulnerable to attacks utilizing firearms, explosives and chemicals. Countermeasures to these threats should be incorporated into evacuation plans. A few examples include: response by armed and uniformed law enforcement personnel for all school emergency evacuations and drills, the use of a go ahead team to sweep evacuation routes and sites, trying to avoid evacuation routes and sites in proximity to parking lots and trash dumpsters and the development of multiple options for building administrators faced with a bomb threat.

Hostage taking

"...a trained negotiator can help to stabilize a hostage situation and thus reduce the chances of injury to hostages..."

Twice utilized by Chechen terrorists, the taking of hostages on a school bus or at a school has been another popular tactic as it creates a situation of ongoing danger for the hostages. This, in turn, can create ongoing media coverage of the incident. And while many schools conduct training for staff on what they should do if taken hostage and even more have protocols for hostage situations in their emergency operations plans, very few are detailed enough to address an incident the scale of the Beslan attack.

Unlike other situations, a teacher, bus driver or administrator who is taken hostage cannot refer to any emergency plan component during the incident. In the event that staff are taken hostage, proper training and individual familiarity with the district's emergency procedures will have to serve as a guide for staff members who are taken hostage. One Georgia school district police department had an officer from each high school and several supervisors trained in hostage negotiations at the Georgia Police Academy. This training would enable an officer skilled in hostage negotiations to arrive at the scene of any school hostage incident in under ten minutes. As a trained negotiator can help to stabilize a hostage situation and thus reduce the chances of injury to hostages, this approach has merit. In a related example, the same police department developed and distributed a guide on what to do in school hostage situations for school administrators.

THE CHEMICAL THREAT

Since September 11, many of our clients have expressed considerable interest in the dangers of chemical and biological incidents of terrorism. A major problem stemming from this interest is that many consultants went on to develop school emergency operations plans that provide one protocol for chemical and biological incidents when, in fact, there are very distinct differences between the two types of incidents. Understanding these differences is crucial in order to prevent, mitigate and prepare for incidents of either type. This is another example of why the backgrounds of consultants should match the work they are retained for. Consultants who are hired to assist in emergency operations plan development should have a strong work experience and training background in the field of emergency management. A career in school security, law enforcement, school administration or mental health and other such disciplines does not adequately prepare someone to coordinate emergency planning. Emergency planning is a specialized field best handled by professionals with an emergency management background.

This section will provide a basic understanding of chemical weapons concerns. We are in no way predicting either type of attack on a school, only trying to help school officials correct the deficiencies in many safe school plans that are now in place. We must also be mindful that schools, school bus routes or a school event could be impacted as incidental targets when a separate primary target is hit.

In this and the following section, we will rely heavily on *Jane's Chemical – Biological Defense Guidebook* which is by far the most comprehensive and respected book on the topic in print. Our editors at Jane's were kind enough to provide us with a copy of the $1,200 book and to grant permission to use it as source material for this book. We will also draw from the *Jane's Unconventional Weapons Response Handbook, Jane's Counter Terrorism, Jane's Chem-bio Handbook, Jane's Safe Schools Planning Guide for All Hazards, School/Law Enforcement Partnerships – A Guide to Police Work in Schools* by Ram Publishing, Michael Dorn's Columns in *School Planning and Management* and *Campus Safety* magazines as well as information provided through numerous interviews with our associated experts.

CHEMICAL ATTACK

The use of chemical weapons dates back to 2000 BC when "Toxic fumes" were employed in India. In more modern times, they have been used by military forces in World War I with devastating effect with an estimated 1.25 million poison gas casualties during the war. Terrorists and others have also made use of chemical weapons in attacks such as the poorly executed, but still deadly and disruptive sarin nerve agent attack on Tokyo subway systems by the Aum Shinriko cult in 1995.

Mass casualty, no-notice chemical attacks are categorized by most experts as low probability but high impact events which have many characteristics that differentiate them from biological attacks. The first major difference is that many types of chemical attacks are easier to carry out since it is less difficult to acquire and use many types of dangerous chemical substances than it is to gain access to biological weapons such as anthrax or smallpox. This availability puts the means to carry out a chemical attack within reach of a broad range of individuals and groups who may wish to orchestrate this kind of attack. However, it is important to note that though such attacks have occurred in recent years they have still remained infrequent.

In a no-notice chemical attack, indications of the attack are typically seen close to the site and time of the attack. Most chemical weapons that are likely to be used produce immediate symptoms (visible within seconds or minutes) in those who are victimized in contrast to many types of

"In a no-notice chemical attack, indications of the attack are typically seen close to the site and time of the attack."

biological attacks where indications of a no-notice attack typically begin to appear over a greater time frame (visible within hours, days or weeks) and often in places remote from the actual attack site. In chemical attacks the initial response is more likely to be made by emergency response personnel who are summoned to the vicinity of the attack(s) whereas the response for biological events is more apt to involve medical and public health officials. Action steps in the emergency operations plan will typically need to address such measures as sheltering in place, mass decontamination of victims, and the rapid establishment of exclusion zones.

There are a variety of substances that could be used for a chemical attack ranging from readily available pesticides or substances like cyanide to deadly nerve agents that are often much harder to acquire such as sarin, tabun or soman. There are also a variety of attack methods that can be used effectively under a wide range of weather conditions. As chemical attacks - particularly those involving fast-acting nerve agents, produce more rapid onset of symptoms the emergency medical response to such incidents must be immediate and effective to minimize the severity of harmful effects on victims.

These types of incidents also require a very careful response by public safety officials to prevent responders themselves from becoming victims as happened in the Tokyo subway attacks. The competing demands of time and the need for precautions in the response pose extreme challenges to emergency personnel. Additionally, it is of critical importance that responders quickly identify the likely agent used in order to facilitate more effective emergency medical care. Fortunately, the ability of emergency response agencies to address this type of attack has improved in recent years through a massive influx of new equipment and superior training of personnel. Through federal terrorism grant funding, far more public safety agencies now have or are obtaining advanced training, protective equipment and devices used to identify deadly chemicals in the field. Understanding the threat of chemical weapons is the first step in deciding what actions are realistic. Local, state, and federal agencies and qualified consultants can provide more detailed and specific guidance as needed.

> "These types of incidents also require a very careful response by public safety officials to prevent responders themselves from becoming victims as happened in the Tokyo subway attacks."

THE BIOLOGICAL THREAT

This section will examine the complex arena of the use of biological weapons as tools of terrorists. An early account of biological warfare occurred in 1346 at Kaffa (now Feodosiya, Ukraine), when the bodies of soldiers who died from the plague were launched by catapult over the walls of the besieged city. In more recent history, Japanese soldiers used biological weapons in their conquest of China in the early 1940's and launched balloons carrying biological agents toward the Western coast of the United States after we entered the war. In 1989, Iraq stockpiled 19,000 liters of botulinum, 8,500 liters of anthrax, 340 liters of clostridium perfingens and 2,500 liters of aflatoxin. There are also grave concerns over the security of the enormous stockpiles of deadly biological agents including smallpox and anthrax accumulated by the Soviet Union before its collapse. Such powerful biological weapons have the potential to cause large numbers of casualties, panic among the affected populace and immense expense and disruption.

For a variety of reasons, there is greatly increased concern over the potential use of biological weapons in the United States in recent years. In 1984 a biological attack left 751 people infected with *Salmonella typhimurium* in Wasco County, Oregon. This attack, coordinated by the leader of a religious commune, Bhagwan Shree Rajneesh, demonstrated our vulnerability to biological attacks. Since that time, intelligence information relating to efforts of domestic and international terrorist groups as well as by rogue nations to develop biological weapons capabilities has contributed to these increased concerns.

While a school or school event could be the release site of a biological attack, other targets are more likely to be selected. The goals, motivations, and capabilities of an individual or group bent on an attack, along with the ease of striking various targets and many other factors play into target selection. An otherwise less desirable target might be chosen because a seemingly ideal target is too well secured to ensure a successful attack.

A number of options are available for those wishing to carry out a biological attack. A no-notice attack could involve the covert release of dried or liquid biological agent, such as a viral, toxin, bacterial, or rickettsial agent against humans, animals, or food products and agricultural goods. Distribution could also be carried out by mailing letters or packages to a school. This type of release could generate symptoms in humans days, if not weeks, after the initial release depending on a series of agent conditions including: amount and type of agent; method of dispersion and delivery; existing environmental conditions and the nature of the selected target. While schools in any community impacted by a biological attack could be affected, an area of particular concern would be a common food source attack. Substances such as botulinin toxin could be used to contaminate food or beverage supplies from a vendor serving numerous schools with deadly and more rapid affect. Prompt detection, identification of the agent and notification of all schools using the contaminated product to prevent further exposure would be critical in minimizing casualties. Unfortunately, school emergency operations plan actions steps developed by some consultants without the assistance of local public health officials do not address this concern at all. However, many of these types of attacks are difficult to carry out successfully in practice.

Like chemical attacks, biological attacks are difficult to prevent in a free society. Counterterrorism efforts including intelligence gathering, target hardening, protection of food sources, ventilation systems and other measures are combined with efforts to mitigate the negative effects of a biological attack. Mitigation efforts include enhanced public health surveillance systems designed to help spot abnormal patterns of illnesses that could be the result of a biological attack and the deployment of the Strategic National Stockpile (which includes emergency medicines) to the affected site. A key to success in addressing a biological attack is early detection and prompt assessment of the situation.

> "A key to success in addressing a biological attack is early detection and prompt assessment of the situation."

DELAYED ONSET OF SYMPTOMS

Unlike a chemical attack, the use of a biological weapon may not be immediately apparent. The response in these instances will not be the lights and siren type of affair that would be expected in a chemical attack. In many scenarios, the shelter in place instructions listed in many school biological incident plans would serve no purpose and could in fact, help increase the effectiveness of an attack. Coordinated response, effective crisis communications and advance training of crisis team members would likely be more critical issues. The public health and medical community along with key government officials are most likely to be involved in response.

As with chemical attacks, government officials and agencies are working diligently to enhance our capabilities to prevent and respond effectively to biological attacks. A side benefit of these efforts is greater protection against natural outbreaks of disease as well. Just as the enormous effort to better equip and train hazardous materials teams to respond to chemical attacks will pay enormous dividends when accidents involving toxic chemicals occur, efforts to protect our populace from biological attack lower risks posed by epidemics and pandemics.

Qualified consulting firms and a variety of government agencies including local and state public health agencies and the Centers for Disease Control provide information and assistance in bolstering prevention and emergency preparedness measures for schools. By making use of public and private sector expertise, school personnel can be better informed and prepared to face the challenges of biological terrorism.

RADIOLOGICAL ATTACK

Probably among the least likely scenarios to be directed at a school target, a radiological attack could take several forms. This type of attack could involve a "dirty bomb" which is a traditional explosive device used to disperse radiological materials. Another type of attack involves the use of simple radiological dispersal. In this scenario, radiological contaminates would be scattered in the target area without the use of explosives or distributed by contaminated food.

The final and most unlikely type of radiological incident involves the use of an actual nuclear device. In this type of attack, devastation is created by a powerful explosion and, second, by dispersal of radiation over a large area – usually near and downwind of the blast site.

"Qualified consulting firms and a variety of government agencies including local and state public health agencies and the Centers for Disease Control provide information and assistance in bolstering prevention and emergency preparedness measures for schools."

While it is probably unlikely that a school would be directly targeted with a radiological attack, the possibility does exist. More importantly, a school in the vicinity of an attack could be affected. This potential means that every safe schools plan should address radiological incidents in the emergency operations plan section.

ELECTROMAGNETIC PULSE/RADIO FREQUENCY DEVICE ATTACK

Like radiological weapons, it is unlikely that this category of weapon would be used to target a school directly, but the use of this type of weapon could impact schools and school transportation in the event a target near a school was selected. Basically, these devices are used to target and shut down electronic based systems such as telephones, radios, computers and electronic ignitions in vehicles. This type of device generates electromagnetic energy to temporarily or permanently damage these types of systems in a manner similar to that achieved when a nuclear detonation creates an electromagnetic pulse. This and other types of threats demonstrate the need for schools not to rely on emergency management planning systems that are totally in electronic format. Though no terrorist attack using this type of weapon has ever occurred, the military development of these types of weapons means that it could be possible for someone outside the military to create a weapon of this type. At least one major technology magazine has run a feature article claiming that such a device could be constructed by civilians at relatively low cost.

USING AN AIRCRAFT AS A WEAPON

While the risk of an aircraft being used to attack a site obviously exists for any type of facility, it is highly unlikely that a school would be directly targeted by this type of attack. Significant damage to a school could likely be achieved with less effort by attacks that would be far easier to accomplish. If an attack on a school using an aircraft were carried out, it would most likely involve the use of a small private plane or commercial aircraft taking off from a regional airport.

FOOD CONTAMINATION THREAT

In an incident that occurred in Florida a few years ago, a middle school student allegedly contaminated salsa in the

"School districts should take adequate precautions to try to prevent accidental or intentional incidents involving contamination of drinking water, cafeteria food, and air."

school's cafeteria with rat poison. As many as fifty students ingested the poison, which is reportedly used in the school for pest control. Fortunately, another student told the school's resource officer what had taken place, the offender was quickly apprehended and students were treated. While some of the students had to be treated at a local hospital, no fatalities occurred.

School districts should take adequate precautions to try to prevent accidental or intentional incidents involving contamination of drinking water, cafeteria food, and air. While preventive measures are not foolproof, they do reduce the chances that a major contamination incident will occur. School emergency operations plans must also outline response and recovery steps should a mass contamination incident take place.

At the same time, school officials should review their existing emergency operations plans with those same officials to ensure that they provide proper guidance for a mass contamination incident. Whether due to an act of terrorism or an accidental contamination, these types of incidents can be very difficult to handle under the best of circumstances, and advance planning can be well worth the effort.

Below are just a few considerations for preventing and planning for mass contamination incidents:

- Conduct an annual site survey of the entire campus. Local public safety, emergency management, and public health officials should be invited to help ensure that potential hazards are discovered.

- Establish policies, procedures, and daily practices to keep food and beverages properly secured and inaccessible to unauthorized individuals.

- Constant attentiveness of buffet style food service areas by staff is also helpful. Review security camera coverage of these areas.

- Ensure that food service areas are staged in accordance with state and federal standards. This will help to reduce opportunity for intentional or accidental contamination.

- Make sure that all chemicals and cleaning products are stored in compliance with health and safety codes to minimize the risk to students and personnel in cross contamination.

- Ensure that material safety data sheets (MSDS) are current, accurate, and on file with the appropriate local fire officials. Make sure that copies are also included in your facilities' emergency evacuation kit.

- See if maintenance personnel can enhance the security of heating and air-conditioning units to make it difficult for someone to access them to spray contaminants into the building. Fencing units in can help make it difficult to get close to them. In some cases, special filters can be added to increase protection for occupants.

- Establish a system to quickly shut down heating and air-conditioning systems to minimize a contamination incident (if appropriate to the situation). If a computer based energy management system is in use, this function can be accomplished rapidly with most systems.

- Have contingency plans in place for evacuation in a mass contamination incident. These plans could include evacuating to a minimum of 3,000 feet from the facility, and moving evacuees to a position that is upwind from the affected site in some cases. In other situations, a lockdown will be utilized to minimize contamination.

- Seek guidance from school food service, public safety, emergency management, and public health officials in preparing your plans.

This section has examined a variety of possible scenarios that range from the extremely unlikely to those that would be more likely to be employed in terrorist attacks on school related targets. As we have seen in attacks like the one in Beslan, terrorists sometimes employ multiple types of weapons such as firearms and explosives in their attacks. An awareness of the possibilities when combined with evaluation of probabilities can help school and emergency response officials develop practical prevention and mitigation measures along with thorough emergency preparedness measures.

Chapter 11

The Emotional Impact of School Related Terrorism on Children

Following loss of life and serious injury, our next primary concern is the emotional impact of these violent events on our children. We all know that witnessing and surviving acts of violence will have an impact on adults, let alone children. This issue is particularly critical when we see that there has been at least somewhat of a tendency to target elementary school children.

In approaching this topic, we decided to interview two of the world's top experts in the field of crisis response and recovery for school children. Both of these experts serve on international crisis response teams and have high level experience in the arenas of school safety as well as actual experience in the field of terrorism from responding to actual events or full time work in government antiterrorism units. Very few people in the United States have this combination of expertise due to the rarity of these types of situations and the only recent staffing of large numbers of government personnel to work full time in the field of antiterrorism.

Marleen Wong serves as the Director of School Crisis and Intervention Unit for the National Center for Child Traumatic Stress at UCLA and Duke University and as the Director of Crisis Counseling and Intervention Services for the Los Angeles Unified School District. Identified by the Wall Street Journal as one of the "architects of school safety programs", she has assisted schools after numerous school shootings, disasters and acts of terrorism as a consultant to the United States Department of Education. The tragedies that she has helped to address include: the 1992 civil unrest, the Northridge earthquake in Los Angeles, the bombing of the Murrah Federal Building in Oklahoma City, school shootings in Springfield, Oregon, Littleton, Colorado, Santee and El Cajon, California and the terrorist attacks in New York City and Washington, D.C. She also served in an advisory capacity to the U.S. Department of Health and Human Services during the beltway sniper shooting spree. Marleen assisted the Educational Directorate of the Department of Defense to support the children of troops deployed to the Iraqi war. Ms. Wong currently serves on the National Academy of Science Institute of Medicine (IOM) Board on Neuroscience and Behavioral Health and was a member of the committee, which published the IOM report "Responding to the Psychological Effects of Terrorism." Ms. Wong has co-authored a number of books including the first and second editions of *Jane's School Safety Handbook, Jane's Safe Schools Planning Guide for All Hazards,* and *Jane's Teachers' Safety Guide.* Ms. Wong also serves as a consultant for the highly regarded Jane's world wide school safety consulting team and is a popular keynote speaker at state, national and international conferences.

Our second expert has a similarly impressive and diverse background. A truly dynamic woman, Sonayia Shepherd (Sony) has seen her career skyrocket in recent years. Though still quite young, Ms. Shepherd has served in a number of government positions of high responsibility. Sony served as an Area School Safety Coordinator and Statewide School Crisis Response and Recovery Specialist for the School Safety Project of the Georgia Emergency Management Agency – Office of the Governor. Working in the largest state school safety center in the United States, Sony had primary responsibility for coordination of crisis response and recovery operations for incidents involving death and trauma for schools in Georgia. She was then appointed as the State Antiterrorism Planner for the State of Georgia and later as the Bioterrorism Exercise Coordinator for the Georgia Department of Public Health. Ms. Shepherd recently accepted a position as a member of a government terrorism response team with global responsibilities. Sony has authored and co-authored sixteen books including: *Jane's Safe Schools Planning Guide for All Hazards, Jane's School Safety Handbook Second Edition, Jane's Teachers' Safety Guide* and the *Jane's Citizen Safety Guide*. Ms. Shepherd also serves as part of the Jane's international consulting team and frequently presents at state, national and international conferences. Ms. Shepherd worked on the design teams for the Boy's and Girl's Clubs of America *Safe on All Sides* interactive CD-ROM training program and the Emergency Operations Planning Template for use by the more than 3,500 Boy's and Girl's Clubs worldwide. Ms. Shepherd is certified in Grant Writing, Adventure Therapy, Play Therapy, Juvenile and Adult Case Management, Managing Aggressive Behaviors, Crisis Intervention and Crisis Counseling. Ms. Shepherd is dually certified in Crisis Intervention through the National Organization for Victim's Assistance (NOVA) and the International Critical Incident Stress Foundation (CISM, Mitchell Model).

The authors especially feel a deep sense of gratitude that these extremely busy experts would take time from their hectic schedules to provide all of the information for this chapter. Without their assistance, this valuable information would not be included in this book.

ALL HAZARDS PLANNING EMPHASIZED

Both of our experts emphasized that as with the other three sections of a safe school plan, the recovery plan should be thought of as a plan appropriate for all types of hazards ranging from the death of a single student or staff member to a mass casualty incident such as an act of terrorism on the scale of the attack in Beslan. A well developed recovery plan implemented by properly trained personnel can effectively address the needs of staff, students and their loved ones no matter how large or traumatic the crisis so long as external resources are lined up in advance for incidents of a large scale. As with the other three plan sections, the recovery process will often not be perfect, but with a carefully developed plan and proper training, the crisis response and recovery team can dramatically reduce the negative impact of any crisis.

> "A well developed recovery plan implemented by properly trained personnel, can effectively address the needs of staff, students and their loved ones no matter how large or traumatic the crisis so long as external resources are lined up in advance for incidents of a large scale."

TYPICAL RESPONSES TO VIOLENT ACTS

Ms. Wong has found that children often respond to acts of violence with shock, disbelief and fear. They experience a sense of insecurity and are afraid that the same kind of violence might happen again. Adolescents can respond with either flight from the situation, i.e., withdrawal and avoidance of school and other students, or with a fight response. If they exhibit the second response, they may become more aggressive as a way to defend against the feeling of fear. Some studies have shown that after an act of mass violence, some high school students increase their use and abuse of alcohol or drugs or engage in risk – taking behavior. If the incident has the affect of changing their outlook and attitudes toward life, they may begin to believe that "nothing matters." When students act on the belief that "life is short", they may begin to use poor judgment and disregard the guidance of respected adults. Some examples of poor judgment include driving recklessly, excessive drinking or engaging in high risk sexual behavior.

She continued that children who have had previous experiences with violence or loss in their lives tend to be more at risk for depression or traumatic stress and require the added support of school counselors, school psychologists or school social workers to aid in their return to school. Some children may even need a referral to a mental health professional in the community.

> "In times of crisis, adults, as role models, play a more critical role than ever."

ADULTS SERVE AS BEHAVIORAL EXAMPLES IN A CRISIS

She stressed that both at home and at school, children look to see how adults around them are reacting. In times of crisis, adults, as role models, play a more critical role than ever. Adults in these circumstances, have the task of taking the "middle road" after a crisis or disaster. They must remain calm and realistic so they neither overreact in a time of danger, nor minimize the seriousness of the situation. What children want most at these times is to know that adults will take care of them and that they are not alone. The feelings of isolation and helplessness can be devastating to children.

> "Parents have a bigger challenge now that there is television and the internet. Parents need to decide how much they want their child to see and experience."
>
> Marleen Wong

THE IMPORTANCE OF PLAN DEVELOPMENT

Ms. Wong emphasized the need for schools to take the time to develop a written recovery plan before tragedy strikes.

As with other sections of the safe schools plan, the recovery plan is necessary for and will serve to address a wide range of incidents under the all hazards approach. Sooner or later, most schools will face some sort of event that can have a significant negative impact on staff and students. She feels that there are several key points that school officials should pay particular attention to while developing the recovery plan:

1. The plan must ensure that staff provides a clear message that they want to know how the crisis has affected students. Teachers and other employees must not ignore or deny the impact that the crisis can have on the school family. Often, adults make the judgment that the incident is "over" because they were not impacted or because they have the coping skills to overcome the fear and anger. Students have neither the emotional maturity nor the life experience from past events necessary to confront disasters and violence in the same way as adults. They will need a high level of support that should be formally communicated to school employees through the written recovery plan.

2. The plan should outline how crisis counseling will be available for and provided to students who request it in the aftermath of an incident. Community partnerships should be created in advance and spelled out in the recovery plan. As with emergency operations planning, the period immediately following a crisis is not the time to begin developing a plan of action for these critical services. Community partnerships are of critical importance to private schools and school systems that do not have counselors, school social workers and psychologists on staff or that do not have adequate staffing of mental health personnel.

3. The plan should detail how crisis counseling resources that are available to students, staff and parents can be accessed and it should do so in a manner that makes these services easy to use.

4. Finally, school personnel who are developing and overseeing the implementation of the recovery plan must be aware of how the crisis affects them. The plan

"Parents may want to limit the programs that their children see and be available when "breaking news" interrupts a family program. These news briefs can contain shocking and frightening information and pictures."
Marleen Wong
Director of School Crisis and Intervention at the National Center for Child Traumatic Stress

should stipulate measures to remind crisis response and recovery team members to take the time to address their own needs. This is of critical importance as, like public safety officials, school crisis response and recovery team members will often work themselves beyond their physical and emotional limits after a crisis due to their desire to help children in need. When this occurs, they not only do themselves harm, but cannot serve the children effectively.

The impact of television and other media on children

Sony Shepherd affirms the recommendations made by Ms. Wong. She also pointed out that in some cases, television coverage and information coming to children from other sources could have an impact on children who were not even directly impacted by the crisis event. As an example, both Wong and Shepherd have pointed out in their conference presentations that many children across the nation showed signs of traumatic stress reactions from the events of September 11, 2001. Shepherd emphasized that traumatic stress reactions can result from:

- Seeing the event;

- Hearing about the event and;

- Experiencing the event.

This exposure can come from television coverage, particularly when children watch hours and hours of news coverage of an event such as a multiple victim school shooting or an act of terrorism, particularly one involving children as victims.

RECOVERY IN ACCORDANCE WITH THE U.S. DEPARTMENT OF EDUCATION MODEL

Ms. Shepherd also agreed that schools should have a written recovery plan fashioned in accordance with the United States Department of Education model. Like Ms. Wong, she stressed the need to identify school system and community resources while the plan is being written and that it is crucial that the plan be developed prior to the occurrence of a major crisis. A major concern is that schools are just as responsible for mental health services that are delivered following a crisis as they are for more routine matters. For example, if an individual shows up following a crisis and claims to be a psychologist, school officials may face significant civil liability and tremendous loss of public confidence should this person turn out to be an imposter. Most importantly, this type of situation could result in even more harm to the emotional well being of the children they are allowed to have contact with. This is a very serious problem as a number of individuals have shown up after major crisis events and falsely represented their credentials in order to become a participant. In one case, a convicted child molester showed up during a search for a missing child and claimed to be an employee of a state emergency management agency. This individual was wearing a t-shirt with the agency logo that had been obtained from someone who had attended a conference hosted by the agency. Another individual showed up immediately following a multiple victim school shooting and tried to make school officials believe that he was a federal law enforcement official. It turned out that he was a consultant who was trying to insert himself into the crisis so he could say that he was part of the incident response.

IMPORTANT ASPECTS OF A RECOVERY PLAN

Ms. Shepherd feels that there are certain aspects of the recovery plan that are important for a well rounded recovery effort:

1. The plan must state which crisis response and recovery model will be used throughout the school or district.

2. The plan must list who will serve on the crisis response and recovery team and what their responsibilities are.

3. The plan must address how school crisis response and recovery teams will deal with individual tragedies that occur at and away from the school such as the death of a student or teacher.

4. The plan must address how recovery services will be delivered in the event of a mass casualty event. Mass casualty events require a significant effort under extremely challenging conditions and resources beyond the internal capabilities of most school systems.

How does one diagnose the intensity of the pain, the fears, the anxiety? At first, we huddled together, held hands, cried together, and sought refuge with those who knew what the feelings were about. As time went on, some students sought refuge in their families, in counseling, in painting, in knitting, in God. Still, there were those who sought "healing" means that served to hurt them more than heal."
Ada Dolch
United States Department of Education adjunct trainer and former Principal for the High School for Leadership and Public Service located a few hundred yards from ground zero.

5. The plan should be especially well thought out and detailed when it comes to crisis response and recovery efforts initiated at the family reunification center. For many students and family members, this will be the first opportunity to receive information on crisis counseling services and indicators of traumatic stress reactions that may be seen following the crisis. Due to the large number of people, high emotions and often relatively short time span of this process, careful pre-planning is required for success.

6. The plan should include specific classroom recovery activities that the Crisis Response Team can distribute to teachers. These activities must be on hand in sufficient quantities when the team activates.

7. The plan should outline the types of crisis counseling and crisis intervention techniques that will be used when the team is activated.

RECOVERY PLANNING REQUIRES PROPER TRAINING
Ms. Shepherd pointed out that a proper recovery plan is easier to write than an emergency operations plan, but typically requires more training of Crisis Response and Recovery Team members to adequately prepare them to deliver high quality services. She further advises that, as with the emergency operations plan, the plan should be tailored to fit local conditions and that a good quality planning template can help to achieve this aim with far less staff time than starting from scratch. She cautions school officials desiring to use consultants to select them with great care as there are a number of individuals working in the field without proper credentials and experience and at least one very heavily booked consultant who does not possess the doctoral degree that he claims to have.

RECOVERY – A CRITICAL PHASE OF SAFE SCHOOL PLANNING
Both of our experts agree that no school system or private school can afford to ignore this critical part of safe school planning. Given their extensive level of professional development and vast experience in handling both large and small incidents, school officials would be wise to heed their sage

advice and prepare themselves to lead students, staff and loved ones down the long and hard road to recovery should any type of crisis impact their schools.

Chapter 12

The Political Impact
of Terrorism

Terrorists often hope to affect some form of social change. Lacking the traditional forms of influence like political power, military strength or popular support, they try to utilize limited resources to attack those groups who have these forms of power and influence. One means for terrorists to achieve these types of goals is to use the type, timing and form of an attack in a manner that is calculated to cause significant problems for those in positions of political power.

HOW TO HANDLE TERRORISM – A VOLATILE ISSUE

There is, perhaps, no better example of terrorism's political impact than the current situation where many nations have worked in a coordinated manner with varying degrees of commitment to engage in efforts to combat it. Debates concerning the strategies employed, their effectiveness and handling of specific incidents along with the justification and focus of these efforts have raged in a number of countries. These types of debates have raged extensively in our own nation even though the efforts resulted from the most horrid acts of terrorism of our time. Terrorism is an emotional and volatile issue. The very nature of terrorism can easily create situations where our focus quickly shifts from the core issue of the terrible actions of terrorists to close examination of the efficiency of government in dealing with the problem.

"There is, perhaps, no better example of terrorism's political impact than the current situation where many nations have worked in a coordinated manner with varying degrees of commitment to engage in efforts to combat it."

THE POLITICAL IMPACT OF TERRORISM

While elected officials are not and should not be above criticism and review, terrorists have sometimes gained leverage in the form of political fallout following their attacks. The recent events of terrorism on March 11, 2004 surely caused great concerns for popularly elected leaders of free nations everywhere. While it is impossible to gauge exactly the effect of the Madrid train bombings, which killed 191 people, few would argue that the incident did not influence the election. The subsequent pullout of Spanish troops from the Middle East is an example of societal change connected to political ramifications caused by successful terrorist attacks.

While these points probably seem rather obvious to even casual observers of world events, it is important to remember that school-related terrorism can have the same type of consequences as other, more common, types of terrorist attacks. This is another area where the type of disinformation concerning schools and terrorism that has been so common in our nation since September 11, 2001 can have an adverse impact on the political process in free countries such as our own. There have been those who hold themselves out as experts on school terrorism who have painted an inaccurate picture that state and federal government agencies have done relatively little to address the concerns relating to terrorism and schools. Having been involved with a number of state and federal government efforts designed to help make our schools safer from terrorism and other hazards, we find some of these criticisms to have little merit or basis. There have been and are numerous state and federal government efforts that can help schools work to address issues relating to terrorism. A survey of the appendix will quickly reveal a number of agencies that can provide information, training and assistance to schools and their community partners.

"If in the 70's terrorism was seen as a tactic to achieve some sort of limited end, it has moved to become a strategy. Terrorism is a convenient device that is now both a means and an end."
Dr. Robert Friedmann

THE BURDEN OF GOVERNMENTAL RESPONSIBILITY

Government officials and agencies must provide assistance and support to a wide range of potential targets of terrorism such as government buildings, commercial and regional airports, port authorities, historical landmarks, food distribution centers and mass transit systems. They must also use available intelligence information and the results of vulnerability assessments to try to evaluate which types of attacks on a variety of potential targets could do our nation the most harm. As with other nations that have concerns of terrorism, the efforts to address these difficult issues will not be perfect. And just like other countries, available resources are finite even for an issue as grave as terrorism.

Each of these issues makes the government's task of addressing terrorism an even more difficult and daunting one. School officials who work with local, state and federal agencies should understand that their personnel are typically very concerned with the safety of our schools and school children. At the same time, these agencies must serve a variety of other organizations that request assistance.

EFFECTIVE HANDLING OF PUBLIC INTERVIEWS AND COMMUNICATIONS

It is important that we understand that our concerns about terrorism will be with us for a long time. Those who are involved with safe school planning must understand that a school does not have to be impacted by an act of terrorism to have a role in helping to minimize the impact of terrorism on our schools. For example, it has been very common in recent years for local media to interview local public safety and school officials about terrorism and schools. It is very important for local officials to handle these and other communications with the public properly by communicating that schools and local emergency responders have given appropriate and thoughtful attention to the issue. By emphasizing the multidisciplinary efforts to develop a comprehensive safe schools plan in accordance with the best practices model provided by the U.S. Department of Education, school and public safety officials can do much to reassure students, staff and the public.

This emphasis is important when we remember that terrorism, by nature, typically involves the use of violence to make people feel a level of fear that is greater than the reality of the danger that terrorists pose. Again, our reactions to terrorism can be far more damaging if we lack coordination and forethought. Understanding how schools can be thrown into the mix of terrorism even when no incident has occurred is

> "Terrorism has moved now to being a threat to the world of a level that is unknown and unprecedented in world history. With the success in changing the government in Spain, terrorists know that this tactic will work to change government."
> Dr. Robert Friedmann

important to our review of this topic. As with other aspects of school-related terrorism, a calm, measured approach that couches antiterrorism efforts in the context of overall safety measures is likely the most appropriate message.

Conclusion

We have taken a direct and no nonsense look at the history of school related terrorism. Starting in 1968 in the State of Israel and finishing with the recent atrocities committed against innocent children, teachers, and parents at a school in Russia and the bombing of a Muslim elementary school in Holland, we have painted as accurate a picture of past instances of terrorism impacting schools as we can while presenting them in the context of terrorism as a whole, emphasizing how rare it is for terrorists to target school children.

We have also examined some of reasons that terrorists have, on these rare occasions, attacked schools as well as why they may, at times, be reluctant to cross a significant line by targeting school children. Looking at the motivations of terrorists who chose school related targets can help us understand certain critical aspects of preparedness activities that can help minimize the achievement of their aims if and when terrorists carry out an attack on a school.

We have talked about the importance of the manner in which school, public safety, government officials and the public react to incidents of terrorism with the same focus – undermining the goals of terrorists.

We took a hard look at one of the most commonly chosen school related and vulnerable targets – the yellow school bus. Focusing on the efforts that government officials and pupil transportation professionals have been engaged in during recent years may help provide assurances that our nation stands ready to adapt enhanced measures should a heightened threat level someday exist.

We discussed, in more detail than any other topic covered, those positive actions that schools and their many community partners can implement to more effectively prevent and mitigate, prepare for, respond to and recover from acts of terrorism. Explaining that this can be accomplished within the framework of measures that should be in place for other more commonly experienced hazards, we emphasized the need to follow carefully developed best practices developed both by public sector agencies like the United States Department of Education and by reputable high quality private sector organizations. We also surveyed the significant damage done to our schools and the public and, in effect, assistance provided to terrorist organizations by those who give incorrect and even dangerous advice and make baseless predictions in the media without the benefit of actual intelligence information, work experience, training or having responded to acts of terrorism.

We looked at the types of methods that have been utilized in school related attacks, other settings and at the types of incidents that may or may not ever unfold with the caution that not only possibilities, but probabilities should be considered. Not designed in any way to predict future events, this section provides considerations for development of a comprehensive safe schools plan. As Chief David Friedberg from Hillsboro County Florida Schools, points out, if an act is foreseeable, appropriate steps can be taken to prepare for it. This section is designed to help officials spot common and serious flaws in safe schools plans such as plans that place chemical, biological and radiological incidents into the same category. By examining concepts like chemical, biological, radiological and other unconventional weapons along with much more common and easy to use weapons like explosives, school and public safety officials can develop much more reliable and effective safe schools plans. Hopefully, the information on these unconventional weapons will also dispel some of the incorrect information that has been disseminated in the past.

We outlined some of the key concerns relating to the emotional well-being of children by mental health professionals who not only have solid credentials, but also have actual experience in the fields of mental health recovery operations for schools and terrorism. Understanding how children are impacted by acts of terrorism, whether they actually witness the event or are exposed to repeated exposure to media reports, is crucial to our efforts to minimize the impact of these events upon our children.

We then took a brief look at the political implications of terrorism and school related terrorism in particular. Understanding that acts of terrorism are often designed to influence the political process of the victimized nation and affect social change is important when one tries to understand the implications of these terrible acts.

Each of these topics was addressed with a goal in mind – to accurately inform the reader of the potential dangers of school related terrorism so they can have a balanced view of the subject without the alarmist fanfare that has been so prevalent in the media. This approach was emphasized because it is crucial that those who have a vested interest in school safety understand that the consequences of a terrorist act are serious enough to take reasonable steps to prepare for it, but the likelihood of such events is low enough that precious resources might, in many cases, be better utilized for more pressing and likely hazards. For example, a school system that has experienced several weapons assaults may need to focus efforts on this known hazard rather than expend them on measures designed to guard against terrorism scenarios that are extremely unlikely.

We very much appreciate the reader's dedication. Taking an hour or two of your busy schedule to better understand this complex and difficult subject demonstrates your commitment to our most precious natural resource, our children. We wish you the best in your efforts to make the world a better place – one in which the world's children can flourish without fear of harm or violence.

Appendix

There are an impressive number of resources available to schools in need of such assistance. Below is a list of references, agencies and source materials that can provide you with information on how to prepare, prevent, or plan for school emergencies.

Agencies that may be of assistance

State and Federal Agencies

United States Department of Homeland Security (DHS)
For campus officials, most of the relevant resources and information available will be geared toward antiterrorism efforts. DHS information and materials are provided at www.dhs.gov.

Federal Emergency Management Agency (FEMA)
The lead federal agency for emergency preparedness, FEMA can provide a wide range of federally funded training, free online training programs and information. Many of the online training programs are thoroughly detailed independent study programs focusing on emergency preparedness. For more information go to www.fema.gov.

Bureau of Alcohol, Tobacco and Firearms (BATF)
The BATF provides excellent free information, manuals, technical assistance and training concerning bomb threats and explosives. Co-author Michael Dorn served as technical advisor for a BATF/United States Department of Education partnership project which involved the development of an interactive CD ROM bomb threat training program for schools that was released in 2002. This tool is available at no cost to school and law enforcement agencies at www.atf.gov.

Centers for Disease Control and Prevention (CDC)
The CDC provides excellent information concerning bioterrorism. For more information go to www.cdc.gov.

Department of Health and Human Services
This agency also provides information relating to bioterrorism issues. For more information go to www.dhhs.gov.

State Police

In many states, state police personnel can provide free training and technical assistance, as well as provide tactical response support to actual incidents of terrorism.

State Emergency Management Agencies

State emergency management agencies, in most states, can provide free technical assistance, assist with the development of emergency operations plans, aid in coordinating, conducting and evaluating emergency drills and exercises and will respond to provide support following incidents. To find your state point of contact, visit the web site of the National Emergency Management Association at www.nemaweb.org.

State Public Health Agencies

State public health agencies can often provide free training and technical assistance relating to bioterrorism issues.

Local Agencies

While local public safety, public health and emergency management agencies will respond to incidents of terrorism, they can also be a powerful ally in helping campus officials prevent and prepare for acts of terrorism. In many communities, the following types of local agencies can provide excellent assistance:

Local law enforcement agencies

Can provide assistance in emergency operations planning, preventive efforts, and in many cases training for staff.

Local emergency management agencies

Local emergency management officials can assist with hazard analysis, emergency preplanning, emergency operations planning, drills and exercises.

Public health agencies

These agencies often can provide training and technical assistance relating to bioterrorism as well as naturally occurring biological and accidental contamination incidents.

Fire departments

Frequently, fire service personnel can provide excellent training and technical assistance in a variety of areas.

Of particular concern are topics relating to incident command and hazardous materials.

Emergency medical services
Like the other agencies listed in this section, emergency medical services personnel can be a tremendous asset in planning, particularly when planning for mass casualty incidents.

Coroner /medical examiner
A representative from this field can also provide valuable input when planning for mass casualty situations.

PRIVATE SERVICES AND NON PROFIT ORGANIZATIONS

Consultant services
While government agencies provide a wealth of free resources, private trainers, consultants, and subject matter experts can sometimes offer superior services along with more in-depth technical assistance. As with government resources, private service providers should be selected with care. While a few private service providers have expertise in multiple fields, the authors have not encountered any with viable expertise in all of the areas listed above.

Non profit organizations
There are numerous non profit organizations capable of providing excellent training, technical assistance, and response support. Nationally recognized examples include the American Red Cross (www.redcross.org), the International Critical Incident Stress Foundation (www.icisf.org), and the National Organization for Victim's Assistance (www.trynova.org).

DEPARTMENT OF EDUCATION TERRORISM WARNING
According to Department of Education reports, the Education Department recently advised school leaders nationwide to look for people spying on their buildings or buses, or other suspicious activity, to help detect potential acts of terrorism like the deadly school siege in Russia.

This warning follows a recent analysis by FBI and Homeland Security Department personnel of the siege that killed nearly 340 people, many of them students, in the city of Beslan in the fall of 2004.

Deputy Education Secretary Eugene Hickok stated in a letter sent Wednesday to schools and education groups that "the horror of this attack may have created significant anxiety in our own country among parents, students, faculty, staff and other community members."

Department of Education guidance is based on lessons learned following the Beslan siege. Yet there is no specific information pointing toward a terrorist threat to any schools or universities within the United States, Hickok noted.

Federal law enforcement officials also have urged local police to stay in communication with school officials and have asked staff or bystanders to report suspicious activities.

Specifically, schools were told to watch for actions that may be legitimate in isolated instances — but may suggest a threat if many of them happen at one place over a short period of time.

Such suspicious activity includes:

- Attempts to obtain attendance lists, bus routes, as well as site plans for schools.

- Continued surveillance by people disguised as bystanders such as panhandlers, shoe shiners, vendors or street sweepers not seen in the area before.

- Persons observing security drills.

- Persons staring at or quickly looking away from employees or vehicles as they enter or leave parking areas.

- Foot surveillance of campuses involving individuals working together.

This effort is the latest by the Education Department and other federal agencies to encourage school officials to maintain and practice an all hazards plan for responding to emergencies.

According to former Homeland Security Secretary Tom Ridge, following the terrorist takeover of the Russian school in Beslan, President Bush asked his top aides to review plans for dealing with hostage situations.

Schools are being advised to take steps to improve the security of their buildings. Such steps may include installing locks for all doors and windows, having a single entry point into buildings and ensuring school bus drivers are accessible in the event of an emergency.

For more information visit the Education Department crisis planning help site at: http://www.ed.gov/emergency-plan/

SOURCES

ABC News reports of the November 2000 bombing of a school bus in Kfar Darom.

Report of a suicide bomber's detonation at a school in Jersualem in September of 2001. <www.ananova.com>

Associated Press reports of the September 2001 attacks.

Associated Press, Reuters, Agence France Presse May 1994 Chechen Guerilla attacks.

Associated Press, United Press International. June 2002.

"Anatol Lieven on Muslim Reactions to Recent Terrorism" <http://www.carnegieendowment.org/publications/index. cfm?fa=view&id=15927>

BBC News reports of 1998 Algiers bombing.

CNN and the Associated Press. September of 2004.

CNN news reports April 1995 Murrah Federal Building Bombing reports.

C. J. Chivers "Russian Tragedy: 52 hours of fear." Atlanta Journal-Constitution 5 Sept. 2004: A1.

Dr. Robert Friedmann, Georgia State University Department of Criminal Justice - from his presentation at the 2003 Georgia School Safety and Terrorism Conference

Indio, California Police Department *Active Shooter/Rapid Deployment Training Program.* Report of 1999 shooting at a Jewish Childcare center in Los Angeles

Ingram, Judith. "Putin Threatens Preventative Terror Actions." Associated Press 17 Sept. 2004. <http://news. yahoo.com>.

Jane's Chem-bio Handbook, 2002, Jane's Information Group, Coulsdon, Surry, UK.

Jane's Chemical and Biological Defense Guidebook, 1999, Jane's Information Group, Coulsdon, Surry, UK.

Jane's Safe Schools Planning Guide For All Hazards, 2004, Jane's Information Group, Coulsdon, Surry, UK.

Jane's School Safety Handbook, 2004, Jane's Information Group, Coulsdon, Surry, UK.

Jane's Teacher's Safety Guide, 2004, Jane's Information Group, Coulsdon, Surry, UK.

Making the Nation Safer, 2002, The National Research Council, The National Academy of Sciences, Washington, DC.

March or Die – France and the Foreign Legion by Tony Geraghty. Grafton Books, Great Britain, 2001.

New York Times, Washington Post, Associated Press. August 2002.

Practical Information on Crisis Planning: A Guide for Schools and Communities, 2003, Department of Education, Washington, DC.

When Angels Intervene: The Cokeville, Wyoming Bombing Incident, by Hartt Wixom and Judene Wixom, Cedar Fort, 1994.

The Community Response Crisis Team Training Manual – Second Edition Published by the National Organization for Victim Assistance®.

The Interdisciplinary Center – Herzliya, Middle Eastern Times report of Israeli school girls who were shot to death by a Jordanian soldier.

Turkish Ministry of Foreign Affairs, Reports on the PKK.

War on Freedom – How and Why America was Attacked, by Nafeez Moasaddeq Ahmed, The Institute for Policy Research and Development, Tree of Life Publications, Joshua Tree, California, 2002.

Weakfish: Bullying Through the Eyes of a Child, 2003, Safe Havens International, Macon, GA.

Account of the 1993 World Trade Center bombing from Wikipedia. <en.wikipedia.org>

Index

NOTES

NOTES

NOTES

NOTES

For more on the dynamic and information packed presentations
by Michael and Chris Dorn,
email schoolsafety@janes.com,
call 1-800-824-0768 or
visit our website at www.schoolterrorism.com